# BUILD IT
# TOGETHER

## 30 Easy Woodworking Projects
## for Kids and Adults

# BUILD IT TOGETHER

## 30 Easy Woodworking Projects for Kids and Adults

Katie and Gene Hamilton

STACKPOLE
BOOKS

Published by
STACKPOLE BOOKS
5067 Ritter Road
Mechanicsburg, PA 17055

Printed in the United States of America

10 9 8 7 6 5 4 3 2 1

First Edition

A different version of this book was previously
published as *Build It Together: 27 Easy-to-Make
Woodworking Projects for Adults and Children*

*Cover models: Gary and Katie Radziewicz*

*Cover and interior photographs by the authors*

Library of Congress Cataloging-in-Publication Data

Hamilton, Katie.
    Build it together : 30 easy woodworking projects
  for kids and adults / Katie and Gene Hamilton.
      p.     cm.
    Rev. ed. of : Build it together : twenty-seven
  easy-to-make woodworking projects for adults and
  children. 1984.
    ISBN 0-8117-2421-2
    1. Wordwork.   I. Hamilton, Gene.   II. Title.
TT185.H318   1994
684'.08—dc20                              94-2505
                                             CIP

# CONTENTS

# ACKNOWLEDGMENTS

We'd like to thank all the kids and their parents and grandparents who participated and helped us design and build these projects. We hope our readers enjoy working together on these projects as much as we did.

# INTRODUCTION

Welcome to our workshop and the world of woodworking.

Here we've designed thirty simple-to-make woodworking projects for an adult and child to build together. It's rewarding to make something from a piece of wood, and the satisfaction of doing it with someone special makes it even more fun.

All the projects in this book are designed for beginners, people with little or no experience in woodworking. You don't need a fancy workshop and expensive power tools. Our projects can be built with hand tools on a kitchen counter or Ping-Pong table. The materials are easy-to-find dimensional lumber available at home centers and lumberyards.

For each project we have estimated the amount of time you can expect to spend building it and have provided a shopping list for materials. And, of course, we caution you about safety while working with wood. Always wear a pair of safety glasses or goggles to protect your eyes when using a striking or cutting tool like a hammer or a saw.

Although the projects are easy to build, you should read the instructions and carefully look over the illustrated building plan to see how the parts go together. Refer to the Shopping List so that you'll know exactly what's needed to build a project, and study the Cutting List that refers to the Building Plan. It specifies the name of each part, what material it is made of, its size and actual measurement, and how many are used for each project. It gives the exact size of each piece of wood. When you are cutting out pieces of wood for parts, measure twice and cut once.

An important point to know about dimensional lumber is that the nominal size is not its actual size. For example, a 1×3 piece of lumber listed in the Shopping List actually measures only 3/4 by 2 1/2 inches. Wood is measured before it is milled smooth and dried, which reduces its overall thickness by about 1/2 inch.

We parent-and-kid-tested each design on our friends, neighbors, and relatives, and sometimes they helped us with the idea for a project or the design itself. It was a team effort all the way, and that's what this book is about. We hope that kids and their parents, grandparents, aunts, uncles, neighbors, friends, teachers, or scout leaders find projects they want to build and then get right to it and enjoy the wonderful fun of building something together.

# BASICS OF WOODWORKING WITH KIDS

The first time you work with young apprentices, choose a project that's fun and appealing to get them hooked. Save complicated things for down the road. You want this joint venture to be the first of many, so choose a project that they want to build. Because kids like to see the fruits of their labor, start with a small project to keep the work time short and sweet. Be realistic about what you are comfortable doing and can accomplish in a short period of time.

From a little kid's perspective, woodworking does a lot to stimulate the senses. The smell of freshly cut wood and the sound of a saw going through wood add up to a pleasant experience.

Don't saddle a budding carpenter with hard work like cutting through hardwood or the drudgery of a time-consuming task like sanding a large surface. Use inexpensive pine scraps or boards that require less muscle to cut through. You want to encourage children to enjoy woodworking so that they'll want to come back for more. Make it easy and enjoyable in the beginning, and as they learn new skills and master techniques, they'll be proud of their progress.

## Follow a Plan

Look over the building plan for the project, and talk through the steps. Kids like to know what to expect, and breaking the construction process into small, easy-to-complete steps can make a project seem less overwhelming and more fun. A knowledge of what is expected helps kids get an idea of what will be happening next, and this is important when starting a project that may require several hours for glue or finish to dry. Having a framework to follow also helps kids to visualize what the finished project will look like.

## Teach, Don't Preach

Try not to lecture when you're explaining things to a kid. For example, go through the process of sanding, explain why it is necessary to sand and how to do it, but avoid a lecture on the history of sandpaper. You don't want your teammate to lose interest or feel defeated. A fun project can change into a chore for a kid with a short attention span. Keep the project moving, and explain as you work how and why certain pieces go together. Remember, you're working with a kid, not an adult. Don't bore him with details; he'd rather be banging it together than listening to a speech.

When you're working together, you have a unique opportunity to teach children much more than just woodworking skills. You can teach them about life. While you're doing quiet work, like applying glue to joinery or planing off some wood to make a part fit, why not talk about projects you built (or wish you had built) as a kid? Kids love to hear anecdotes from us "old folks" about when we were kids, and this close and quiet time provides the opportunity.

### Fast Finishing Tips

When building your first project with a kid, choose a finishing technique that looks good and takes little time to apply. Avoid paint and other finishes that require a brush, because they can be messy and require lots of cleanup time. These types of finishes also require a long drying time between coats. We like to use spray paint or natural, wipe-on paste or oil finishes. With a wipe-on finish, all you need is a rag to apply it, and there's no danger of drip marks or uneven coverage.

Kids love to see their name in print, so consider using a set of letter stencils and spray paint to personalize a project. Depending on the project, it might be appropriate to stencil large block letters in plain view or to use small letters or carve or write initials on the bottom of a piece to identify the craftsman.

Putting the piece in a vise or on top of a block of wood can make it easy to finish a woodworking project in one setting. In this way, the entire project is raised up from the work surface and can be finished at one time.

### Tools

An **adjustable bevel** is a gauge with a flat, metal blade attached to a wooden handle. By loosening a screw, you can adjust the gauge to any angle. This tool is useful for marking angles on wood.

A **back saw** is a short, fine-toothed saw with a rectangular blade. It is used alone or in a miter box for cutting wood.

A **clamp** is used to hold parts of a woodworking project in position while they are being glued together. There are several types of clamping devices for special purposes. One of the most popular is the C clamp, which is shaped like the letter C and has an adjustable screw on one end for applying pressure.

A **chisel** has a sturdy handle and a blade with a sharp end designed to chip away pieces of wood. It can be used alone or by striking the end of the handle with a mallet to nudge it through the wood.

A **claw hammer** has a metal head with one flat end for striking and the other forked for removing nails. Its handle is made of wood, fiberglass, or steel.

A **combination square** is a 12-inch steel rule attached to a handle with a small level. It is useful for aligning parts accurately before assembling them.

A **compass** is an instrument used to draw arcs or circles or to take measurements. It has two pointed legs connected at one end by a pivot; one leg holds a pencil for marking the curved line.

A **coping saw** has a C-shaped metal frame holding a very thin blade. It is used for making very fine detail cuts in wood.

A **hand drill** looks like an old-fashioned eggbeater and is used to make holes in wood using standard drill bits.

A **keyhole saw** has a curved handle and a long, thin blade. It is used for cutting holes and curves in wood.

A **miter box** is made of wood and has two sides and a bottom. The sides have matching slots cut at 45- and 90-degree angles. It is used to make angled cuts in wood with precision.

A **nail set** is a small, pointed steel shaft used with a hammer to drive nails below the surface of the wood.

A **tape measure** or rule is a retractable flat tape inside a case. It is used for taking measurements.

A **vise** is a mechanical device for holding a piece of wood while you work on it.

## Safety Practices

Most children can safely handle tools with proper supervision. We find that working one-on-one with little kids is especially important because of their need for guidance and supervision. Here are basic guidelines for kids building projects in this book, as well as some general safety advice for kids around a workshop or remodeling project.

- Insist that kids wear safety goggles to protect their eyes when nailing, cutting wood, or performing any other task with cutting or striking tools. These goggles are sold at hardware stores and home centers for under $2, and kids love to wear them.
- It's better for a kid to use a small-size real tool, such as a ladies' hammer, instead of a toy tool unless you know the toy version is heavily constructed of quality materials.
- Put ear muffs or ear protectors on kids before using loud power tools.
- A bicycle or football helmet is the perfect hard hat for a kid to wear around the workshop or a remodeling job site.
- Give kids a work belt or apron to get in the habit of using one.
- If you're sanding drywall or doing fine sanding, everyone should wear a dust mask.
- Don't ever allow kids to play or work with tools unsupervised.
- Keep all tools stored safely and out of reach, especially those with sharp blades and edges.
- Keep paint and other toxic substances out of reach of young children.

# HANGING PLANT HOLDER

This ribbed basket makes an attractive holder for any plant that needs space to stretch out and grow. It's held up with strong natural jute twine.

Carpenters use a pine molding called parting stop to make windows, but you can use it to make this hanging plant holder. Parting stop is readily available at lumberyards and home centers. It comes in long, narrow pieces, easy to cut and glue together. If your lumberyard doesn't stock parting stop, buy an 8-foot number 2 pine 1×4 and have the yardman rip off three 1/2-inch-thick strips. He might charge a small fee for this service.

You build the frame like a log cabin. It's so easy that very little help is needed from the older member of your carpentry team. The dimensions of our holder are suitable for a 4-inch pot and tray, but construction is simple enough that you can design it to fit whatever size pot you have.

Take a look at the parting stop, and you'll see that it's not square. When you're gluing and nailing ribs together, put glue on the 1/2-inch side of all the ribs. You'll also find that it's easier to drive nails into the ribs before you place them in position. This makes alignment easy and prevents damage to lower ribs from excessive hammering.

You can save time and have a better-looking stain job if you apply the stain before assembly. Other finishes, like paint, should be applied after the holder is tightly glued together.

_____ TIME REQUIRED _____

Four hours for cutting, building, and assembling, plus drying time for glue and finish.

## SHOPPING LIST

| Item | Quantity |
|---|---|
| 3/4″ × 1/2″ × 8′ pine parting stop | 3 |
| number 3 finishing nails | 1 box |
| carpenter's wood glue | small bottle |
| heavy twine or jute | 1 ball |
| plastic plant pot | 1 |
| paint, stain, or other finish | 1 quart |

## CUTTING LIST

| Part | Name | Quantity | Size | Material |
|---|---|---|---|---|
| A | First ribs | 2 | 3/4″ × 1/2″ × 13″ | pine |
| B | Second ribs | 2 | 3/4″ × 1/2″ × 12 1/2″ | pine |
| C | Third ribs | 2 | 3/4″ × 1/2″ × 12″ | pine |
| D | Fourth ribs | 2 | 3/4″ × 1/2″ × 11 1/2″ | pine |
| E | Fifth ribs | 2 | 3/4″ × 1/2″ × 11″ | pine |
| F | Sixth ribs | 2 | 3/4″ × 1/2″ × 10 1/2″ | pine |
| G | Seventh ribs | 2 | 3/4″ × 1/2″ × 10″ | pine |
| H | Eighth ribs | 2 | 3/4″ × 1/2″ × 9 1/2″ | pine |
| I | Ninth ribs | 2 | 3/4″ × 1/2″ × 9″ | pine |
| J | Tenth ribs | 6 | 3/4″ × 1/2″ × 7″ | pine |

Construction of your plant holder begins by cutting the parting stop to length. An inexpensive wooden miter box will help you make square cuts at the ends and improve the appearance of your holder, but it's not required. Using a ruler, mark the length of each set of ribs, and cut them to size, following the Cutting List.

The planter is assembled upside down. Begin with the longest set of ribs (A), and lay them parallel to each other about 10 inches apart. Take the second set (B), and drive number 3 finishing nails into the center of the ribs about l inch from each end. Drive the nails deep enough so that their points begin to come out the backside of the rib. Turn the rib over, and apply a small amount of glue around the area where the

nail points through. Place one of the ribs from the second set on top of the first at a 90-degree angle and with a 1-inch overlap; align them so the nails are centered. Hammer the nails in, then repeat this process with the other ribs.

Check to see whether the first two sets of ribs are square by placing a combination square against one corner. Any piece of cardboard that has a square corner can also be used.

The third layer of ribs is applied in the same way. Place the third set of ribs on the second, align it, with a 1-inch overlap, and mark the spot where you want the nail to go on each end. Remove the rib, and drive nails through the mark until their points just stick out. Do the same to the other ribs in

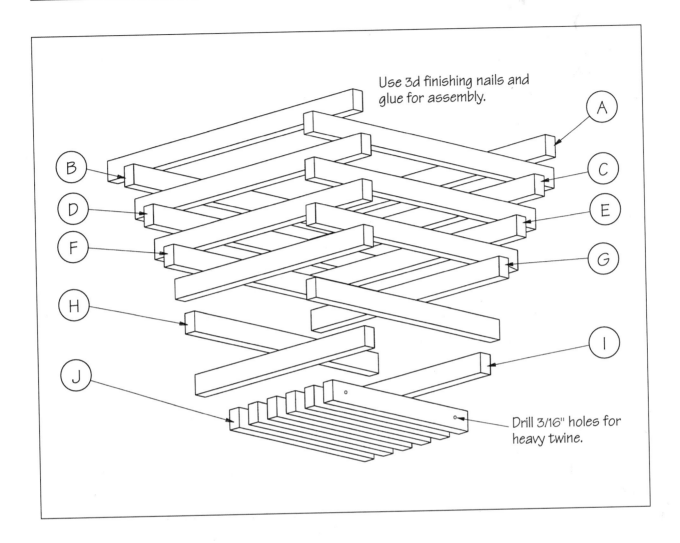

Use 3d finishing nails and glue for assembly.

Drill 3/16" holes for heavy twine.

the third set, putting a drop of glue on the spot where the nail point comes out, and then nail both in place.

Repeat this process with the fourth through ninth sets of ribs. As the holder takes shape, check to see that it's square, and sight down one side to make sure it's not twisted.

The last layer—the bottom of the holder—is made from the six ribs in the tenth set. First drill 3/16-inch holes about 1/2 inch from the ends of the two outside bottom ribs for the hanging twine to pass through. Then arrange all six ribs so they are evenly spaced across the holder's bottom.

Cut two pieces of jute or heavy twine twice the distance that the bottom of the

plant holder will be from its hanging hook. Pass the jute through one of the holes you drilled in the bottom rib, and tie a knot in its end so it can't slip out. Pass the other end through the hole at the opposite end and knot it. Repeat this for the other side. You can also suspend the plant holder with rawhide shoelaces, macramé twine, rope, wire, or cord, and you can add decorative beads if desired.

Finish your holder with a coat of polyurethane varnish, or paint it.

Secure the holder to the ceiling with an adequate anchor. Remember that plants are heavy; use a heavy-duty plastic plaster anchor or an expansion-type anchor rated at fifty pounds or more.

# BIG AND LITTLE TOOLBOXES

Not too long ago, the first project most apprentices completed was a box to hold their tools. Here are two easy-to-construct traditional toolboxes, one scaled for a master craftsman, the other just right for his apprentice.

These matching tool-boxes are constructed from inexpensive but hard-working pine with hardboard bottoms. There is room for long-handled tools such as hammers and saws, plus small items like nails and measuring tape. Your screwdrivers and chisels are stored in custom-made compartments that hold them all in a handy upright position.

Our boxes are sized to be built with standard dimensional lumber with no long ripsaw cuts required. Construction of both toolboxes is identical except for the dimensions. The directions here are for the apprentice box, but you can use them to build the large toolbox by adjusting the measurements given, using the Cutting List as a guide.

Begin by laying out the dimensions of the ends (A), sides (B), nail compartment partitions (D), and divider (E) on the wood (see Cutting List). Use a combination square to draw straight layout lines. Then cut the pieces, securely clamping the wood to a table or placing it in a vise for safe and accurate cutting. When cutting, keep your saw to the waste side of the layout lines. Don't forget to wear safety glasses or goggles whenever you use cutting or striking tools.

The sloping end shoulders of part A are laid out by making a full-size cardboard

TIME REQUIRED

Four hours for cutting, building, and assembling each box, plus drying time for glue and finish.

### SHOPPING LIST: BOTH BOXES

| Item | Quantity |
|---|---|
| 6′ of 1×8 pine | 2 |
| 6′ of 1×4 pine | 2 |
| 24″ × 48″ (quarter sheet) 1/4″ hardboard | 1 |
| number 4 finishing nails | 1 box |
| 1″ roofing nails | 1 box |
| 3/4″ tacks | 1 box |
| heavy shoelaces | 2 laces |
| carpenter's wood glue | small bottle |
| 120-grit sandpaper | 1 sheet |
| paint, stain, or other finish (optional) | 1 quart |

### CUTTING LIST: SMALL BOX

| Part | Name | Quantity | Size | Material |
|---|---|---|---|---|
| A | Ends | 2 | 71/4″ × 71/4″ × 3/4″ | pine |
| B | Sides | 2 | 31/2″ × 18″ × 3/4″ | pine |
| C | Bottom | 1 | 9″ × 18″ × 1/4″ | hardboard |
| D | Nail compartment partitions | 2 | 31/2″ × 3 3/8″ × 3/4″ | pine |
| E | Divider | 1 | 71/4″ × 161/2″ × 3/4″ | pine |

### CUTTING LIST: LARGE BOX

| Part | Name | Quantity | Size | Material |
|---|---|---|---|---|
| A | Ends | 2 | 71/4″ × 71/4″ × 3/4″ | pine |
| B | Sides | 2 | 31/2″ × 24″ × 3/4″ | pine |
| C | Bottom | 1 | 9″ × 24″ × 1/4″ | hardboard |
| D | Nail compartment partitions | 2 | 31/2″ × 3 3/8″ × 3/4″ | pine |
| E | Divider | 1 | 71/2″ × 221/2″ × 3/4″ | pine |

pattern (see Building Plan) and then tracing it on the face of the end. When you clamp part A for cutting, place a piece of scrap wood along the layout line to guide the saw.

The handle slot in the divider (E) is next on the list. Make marks 61/2 inches from each end and 11/4 inches from the top edge. Through these two spots, drill 1-inch holes; these will form the outside corners of the handle. Then use a keyhole or coping saw to make straight cuts from the edge of one hole to the other, parallel to the top edge. Sand the handle cutout smooth with a piece of

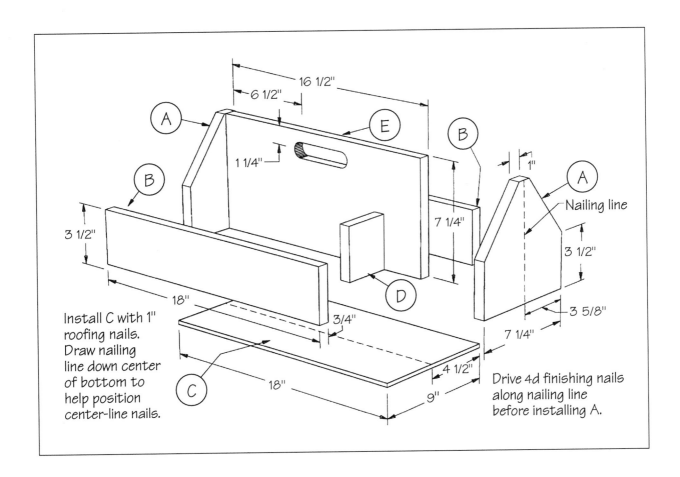

16 1/2"
6 1/2"
A
E
B
A
1 1/4"
B
7 1/4"
1"
Nailing line
3 1/2"
3 1/2"
D
Install C with 1"
roofing nails.
Draw nailing
line down center
of bottom to
help position
center-line nails.
18"
3/4"
3 5/8"
7 1/4"
C
18"
4 1/2"
9"
Drive 4d finishing nails
along nailing line
before installing A.

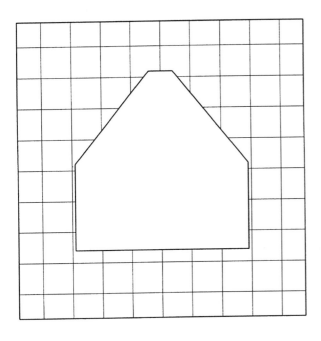

end template
1" squares

120-grit sandpaper wrapped around a short piece of dowel.

Sand all the cutout parts with 120-grit sandpaper. Then test fit the parts, and make any corrections that are needed before assembly. When everything fits, your toolbox is ready to glue up.

Make a light pencil mark down the center of each end piece (A) to help you keep nails aligned. Drive four number 4 finishing nails placed about 1 1/2 inches apart along this line. Pound them in just deep enough so their points emerge from the other side. Then run a bead of carpenter's glue down one end of the divider (E) and align it down the center of one end piece (A). Check that the divider is flush with the bottom of the end piece and then nail it in place. Follow the same procedure for the other end.

Before you glue on the sides, attach the nail compartment partitions (D) to the divider (E). Use number 4 finishing nails and glue in the same manner as above. Then nail and glue on the sides.

The bottom (C) is held in place with 1-inch roofing nails placed about 1 1/2 inches apart. Drill 1/8-inch pilot holes for these nails, then apply glue and nail the bottom in place.

Your new toolbox is now ready for finishing, if desired. We like the natural pine look, but you can finish your box with paint or stain. After the finish has dried, you can customize your toolbox to meet your exact needs by making tool holders out of heavy shoelaces held in place with tacks or staples. Set a tool in place, put the shoelace in position over the tool blade, and tack it down. Keep the shoelace snug but not too tight, so that the tool will be easy to insert. Repeat for each tool.

Now that your apprentice has completed his own toolbox, he'll be ready to tackle the larger box; he might not even need the master to help on this one.

# BALL AND BAT RACK

What better place to stow baseball equipment than this simple-to-build ball and bat rack? Any Little Leaguer can proudly display his or her favorite baseball gear and keep it neatly stored and out of the way. Our rack is designed for two bats and three balls, with pegs for gloves, batting helmets, or caps. It can be expanded to hold enough for a whole team.

The rack is cut from 1×4 pine stock. This wood is actually 3 1/2 inches wide and 3/4 inch thick so all you have to do is cut the wood to length, and nail and glue it together. An inexpensive wooden miter box will help you make square cuts, but it's not necessary.

Begin construction by laying out the bottom (A), back (B), and top (C) on 1×4 stock (see Cutting List). Then cut out each piece. Next, you will drill the holes. An electric drill and hole cutter will make quick work of cutting out these large holes, but this is best left to the older carpenter. If you use a brace and expandable bit, securely clamp the parts to the table, and either carpenter can drill.

First, three holes are drilled in the top piece (C) to hold the baseballs. The centers of these holes are located 1 1/2 inches from the front edge, and 2 1/2 inches from each end and a third one midway. Mark these

TIME REQUIRED

Four hours for cutting, building, and assembling, plus drying time for glue and finish.

SHOPPING LIST

| Item | Quantity |
|---|---|
| 1×4 pine | 4' |
| 3/8" hardwood dowel | 6" |
| number 4 finishing nails | small box |
| carpenter's wood glue | small bottle |
| 120-grit sandpaper | 1 sheet |
| paint, stain, or other finish | 1 pint |

CUTTING LIST

| Part | Name | Quantity | Size | Material |
|---|---|---|---|---|
| A | Bottom | 1 | 3$1/2$" × 12" × 3/4" | pine |
| B | Back | 1 | 3$1/2$" × 12" × 3/4" | pine |
| C | Top | 1 | 3$1/2$" × 12" × 3/4" | pine |
| D | Pegs | 2 | 2$1/2$" × 3/8" | hardwood dowel |

points, and bore a 2-inch hole through each for the baseballs to rest in.

Lay out the two bat slots in the same way. Their center holes are located 1$1/2$ inches from the front edge of the bottom piece (A) and 3 inches from each end. Drill 1$1/2$-inch holes through the layout marks. Use a combination square to draw straight lines from the edges of these holes to the front edge of the bottom piece. Then, using a saw, cut inside these lines to form 1$1/4$-inch slots for the bat handles.

Sand the pieces with 120-grit sandpaper. Round off all edges of the bat slots and baseball holes using sandpaper wrapped around a dowel.

Assembly is easy. Begin by driving four evenly spaced number 4 finishing nails along the back edges of the top and bottom. Drive them through the pieces until just the tip protrudes from the other side.

Next, run a bead of glue down the top edge of the back piece (B). Then, while one member holds the back straight to keep

edges aligned, the other nails on the top. Now turn the rack over, and glue and nail the bottom to the back following the same procedure.

For the glove and hat pegs, drill two 3/8-inch holes in the front edge of the bottom piece 1$1/2$ inches from each end. Drill these holes angling downward so that the dowels, when inserted, will slant upward and prevent your hat and glove from slipping off. Use an adjustable bevel set at a slight angle (5 degrees) to act as a guide. If you don't have a bevel, cut a piece of cardboard to a 5-degree angle, and use it as a guide.

Turn your rack on its back, put a drop of glue in each dowel hole, and tap in 3/8-inch dowels (D). Set the whole works aside for the glue to dry.

Allow the glue to dry overnight, then use a nail set to sink the heads of the finishing nails below the wood surface. Scrape off any excess glue with a chisel, and give the rack a final sanding. Then it's ready to stain, paint, or varnish.

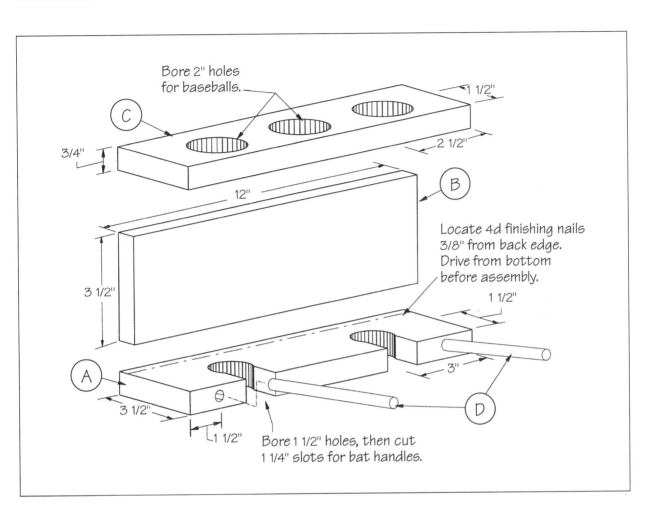

Bore 2" holes
for baseballs.

1 1/2"

C

3/4"

2 1/2"

12"

B

Locate 4d finishing nails
3/8" from back edge.
Drive from bottom
before assembly.

3 1/2"

1 1/2"

A

3"

D

3 1/2"

1 1/2"

Bore 1 1/2" holes, then cut
1 1/4" slots for bat handles.

You can attach your rack to a wall with plastic wall anchors. If you have built a rack with a larger capacity, use expansion-type fasteners. We used large picture-hanging brackets and finishing nails driven into the lath of a plaster wall. If your walls are drywall, use plastic wall anchors. Tighten the anchor screws until their heads are 1/8 inch from the wall surface, then hook the picture brackets over the screw heads.

# KNIFE BLOCK

Even the best knives will lose their edges if not stored properly. Our knife block offers knives protection and makes a wonderful gift. This block is sure to put a smile on the face of any chef and will handsomely grace the fanciest of kitchens. It looks expensive, but it isn't, because the design is simple and the block is made of layers of common 1×8 pine boards and lattice glued together. Except for cutting, all of the work can be tackled by an inexperienced apprentice.

The block is 10½ inches high, 5¾ inches wide, and 7½ inches long. It was designed to hold five knives and a sharpening steel, but you can design your knife block to hold more or fewer knives.

All lumberyards stock number 2, 1×8 pine. When shopping for materials, select boards that are flat and knotfree along their edges. Knots in the center of a board are all right since the interior laminates are hidden. If your lumberyard doesn't stock lattice 3¾ inches wide, purchase what is available. You can glue several pieces edge-to-edge to make the 7½ inches width. Please note that you can't have the pieces cut at the lumberyard; they have to be cut after the block is partially assembled.

Measure your knives before you begin cutting; a height of 10½ inches will house

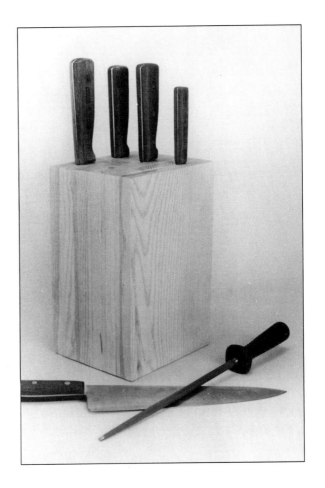

most knives. If you have a large chef or bread knife, change the height of the block to fit it.

Begin construction by cutting 3¾-inch wide lattice into ten 24-inch long pieces. Glue these pieces edge-to-edge to make the

| TIME REQUIRED |
|---|
| Four hours for cutting, building, and assembling, plus drying time for glue and finish. |

## SHOPPING LIST

| Item | Quantity |
|---|---|
| 1×8 pine | 8′ |
| 3 3/4″ pine lattice | 8′ |
| carpenter's wood glue | small bottle |
| number 3 finishing nails | small box |
| 100-grit sanding disk | 3 disks |
| 120-grit sandpaper | 1 sheet |
| mineral oil | 1 pint |

## CUTTING LIST

| Part | Name | Quantity | Size | Material |
|---|---|---|---|---|
| A | Thick pieces | 6 | 7 1/2″ × 10 1/2″ × 3/4″ | pine |
| B | Thin pieces | 5 | 7 1/2″ × 10 1/2″ × 1/4″ | pine lattice |

NOTE: *The cutting for this project cannot be done at the lumberyard. It must be done during construction of the project.*

thin pieces (B), which are 7 1/2 inches wide. Edge gluing longer pieces of lattice together saves time. After the glue is dry, cut these pieces in half to form two B parts.

Gluing the lattice together is easy. Apply glue to the edges of the pieces, and then place four rubber bands around them. Put them on wax paper or aluminum foil, and place a heavy object on top of them. You can stack both assemblies on top of each other to dry, but insert wax paper or foil between the pieces.

While the glue is drying, cut the thick laminate pieces (A) from the 1×8 stock. Use a combination square to draw straight cut lines across the board, and keep your saw cuts to the waste side of this line.

After the glue has dried, cut the thin pieces into five equal sections 10 1/2 inches long. The cutouts for the knives are laid out next. Decide the order in which you want the knives to be arranged in the block, num-

bering each one. Then lay a knife on piece B, and trace around the blade. Do this for all the knives. After tracing all the knives, number the laminate parts so they can be assembled in the right order come gluing time.

Remove the wood inside the knife blade outlines with a coping saw. A saber or jigsaw can also be used. Securely clamp the pieces to the table, or place them in a vise. Have one team member support the wood while the other makes cutouts for the large knives. Don't worry if the piece breaks at the bottom, since it will be glued between two thick pieces of pine.

Gluing up the block is easy but messy. Protect your table with plenty of paper. Begin by selecting a knotfree thick piece for the outside. Place it on the table with its better side facing down. Take the first thin piece with knife blade cutouts, and smear plenty of glue on one side. Put it in place on

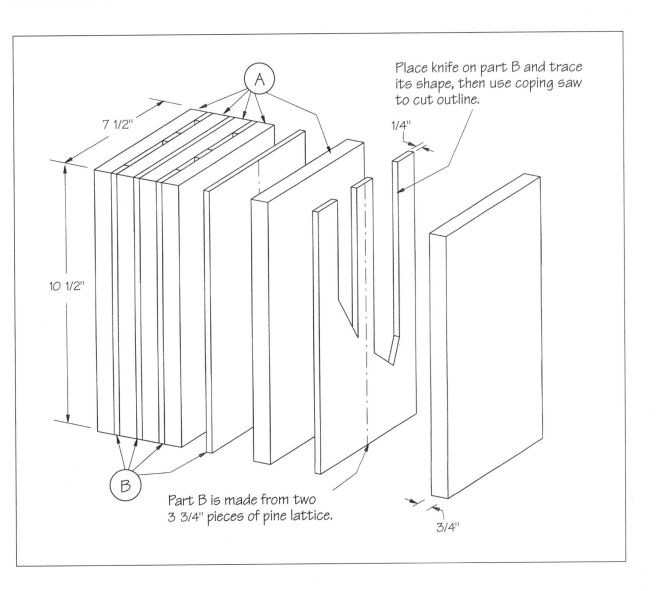

A

Place knife on part B and trace its shape, then use coping saw to cut outline.

7 1/2"

1/4"

10 1/2"

B

Part B is made from two 3 3/4" pieces of pine lattice.

3/4"

top of the thick piece, sliding it around to spread the glue. Then spread glue on its other side, and place the second thick piece over it, again sliding the piece around to spread the glue.

To keep the sandwich in alignment when you are clamping, drive several number 3 finishing nails through the pieces. One team member should hold the pieces in alignment while the other is nailing. Do this after the second thick piece is in place and to each layer thereafter except for the last

laminate piece; don't nail this piece in place, because the nails will show.

You now have a gluey mess. For best results, clamp the laminates together with four bar clamps, making sure the outside laminate pieces are in alignment. Use scrap pieces under the clamp jaws to prevent marring the sides. If you don't have clamps, place the block on its side, and put something heavy on top of it.

After the glue has dried, the block must be sanded smooth. Use an electric hand drill equipped with an inexpensive sanding disk. The older carpenter should take charge of grinding the block. The apprentice can finish the sanding by hand or with an orbital sander. Fill any slight gaps with wood putty, and sand them smooth. Then wipe the dust off, and apply several coats of mineral oil. Mineral oil is nontoxic and a better choice than a toxic finish because the wood surfaces may come in contact with food.

# KITCHEN TRIVET

Our kitchen trivet not only is a useful gift, it's easy to make. This almost instant project is constructed around an inexpensive 8-inch-square ceramic tile with scraps of lumber for its sides. Since there is little cutting for the carpenters to do, this might be a good beginning project for inexperienced adults or young woodworkers to tackle.

Our trivet measures 8 1/2 inches square, but you can make a larger hot plate using several tiles, either two or three in a row to form a rectangle or four to make a large square. The tile you choose can be colorfully painted or glazed a single color. The selection of tiles is endless, so look for ones that match your kitchen, dishes, or table decorations.

The tile sits on a piece of square flakeboard and rests on feet made of furniture tack glides. We chose maple for the sides, but pine lattice, which is less expensive and easier to find, can be substituted.

Begin by laying out the bottom (A) on the piece of flakeboard or plywood. To do this, measure out an 8-inch square, marking the corners. Then connect these marks with straight lines to form a square. Cut along the lines, keeping your saw to the waste side.

To cut the sides (B and C), clamp the maple piece or lattice to the table. Support the ends of the pieces for a square cut as you cut them. An inexpensive miter box helps with these cuts but is not necessary. Measure and cut the two short side pieces

<u>TIME REQUIRED</u>

Two or three hours for cutting, building, and assembling, plus drying time for glue and finish.

<u>SHOPPING LIST</u>

| Item | Quantity |
|---|---|
| 3/4″ × 8″ × 8″ flakeboard or plywood (cut from scrap) | 1 |
| 11/4″ pine lattice or maple | 36″ |
| 8″ × 8″ ceramic tile | 1 |
| tack glides (7/8″ base) | 4 |
| number 3 finishing nails | 1 box |
| carpenter's wood glue | small bottle |
| 120-grit sandpaper | 2 sheets |
| tile mastic, adhesive caulk, or construction adhesive | 2 ounce tube |
| paint, stain, or other finish | 1 pint |

<u>CUTTING LIST</u>

| Part | Name | Quantity | Size | Material |
|---|---|---|---|---|
| A | Bottom | 1 | 8″ × 8″ × 3/4″ | plywood or flakeboard |
| B | Short sides | 2 | 1/4″ × 11/4″ × 8″ | pine lattice or maple |
| C | Long sides | 2 | 1/4″ × 11/4″ × 81/2″ | pine lattice or maple |

(B) to a length of 8 inches. The long sides (C) are cut to 81/2 inches.

You will find it easier to predrive the nails into the side pieces until their points protrude from the backside, before they are glued to the edge of the bottom piece. Space four number 3 finishing nails 2 inches from each end and about 1/4 inch from the bottom of the B and C pieces. If you are using maple for the sides, nailing will be easier if you drill 1/16-inch pilot holes.

Run a bead of glue along one edge of the bottom piece (A), and glue a short side (B) to it. Position the side piece so it is flush with the bottom piece and is aligned at the ends. Drive the nails into the bottom. Repeat the process on the opposite edge of the bottom for the other short side.

The long sides (C) are 1/2 inch longer and will overlap the short sides on the ends.

Place glue on the ends of the short sides (B) to hold the corner joints tight and along the edges of the bottom piece (A), then nail both long sides into place.

Now you're ready to tack on the glides that serve as feet for the trivet. Find their locations on the underside of the bottom by measuring 3/4 inch in from each side. Mark these spots in each corner. The four plastic pads can be nailed directly into the trivet's bottom.

Turn the trivet over and check to see whether the tack glide nails are sticking through the bottom. If they are, hammer them flat, because the points will make the tile lie crooked.

Just about any type of adhesive caulk, construction adhesive, or tile mastic will hold the tile in place. If you use caulk, run a liberal bead around the trivet's base about

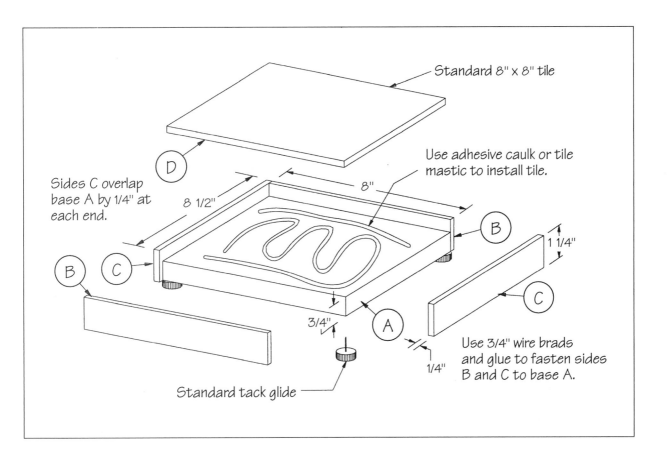

Standard 8" x 8" tile

Use adhesive caulk or tile
mastic to install tile.

Sides C overlap
base A by 1/4" at
each end.

8 1/2"

8"

D

B

B

C

1 1/4"

C

3/4"

A

1/4"

Use 3/4" wire brads
and glue to fasten sides
B and C to base A.

Standard tack glide

an inch from the sides. Apply construction adhesive in the same way, with additional adhesive in the center. Tile mastic is spread with a notched trowel; follow the manufacturer's directions to apply. Be careful when working with any adhesive; they are sticky and will be difficult to remove from wood sides.

After the glue is applied, set the tile in place, and slide it around to spread the glue. Then center the tile, leaving an equal space on all sides. Set the trivet aside to let the glue dry.

When the glue has hardened, sand the sides smooth, and slightly round all the edges with 120-grit sandpaper. Apply a wipe-on finish to protect the wood from food stains, and your trivet is ready for use.

# KEY RACK

Here's a good last-minute gift project. This key rack is easy to build, inexpensive, and just right for almost anyone. We used a scrap piece of pine and letters we found at a craft shop. Small, rubber-coated cup hooks are used to hold the keys, and a foot of chain hangs the key rack from the wall.

You'll be able to purchase most of the materials in one stop at your home center or hardware store. Often you'll find a scrap bin with cutoff pieces of pine and hardwood that would be ideal for this key rack.

Begin building the key rack by cutting the board (A) to size. Our key rack measures 5 inches by 12 inches, but you can make a larger one if you'd like.

With a ruler and pencil, mark the location of your key hooks. They are located 2 inches apart beginning 3/4 inch from the bottom of the board and 2 inches from one end. Drill a 1/8-inch pilot hole through the layout marks.

Drill two more 1/8-inch holes in the top edge of the board 1 inch from each end for the chain screws. Then sand the board and letters with 120-grit sandpaper.

Have one team member apply a small amount of glue to the backs of the letters, while the other spaces them evenly on the face of the board above the holes for the

Two to three hours for cutting, building, and assembling, plus drying time for glue and finish.

SHOPPING LIST

| Item | Quantity |
|---|---|
| 1×6 pine | 14" |
| 2¾" wood letters | as needed |
| brass cup hooks | 5 |
| light brass chain | 12" |
| number 4, ¾" pan-head screws | 2 |
| carpenter's wood glue | small bottle |
| 120-grit sandpaper | 2 sheets |
| paint, stain, or other finish | ½ pint |

CUTTING LIST

| Part | Name | Quantity | Size | Material |
|---|---|---|---|---|
| A | Board | 1 | 5" x 12" x ¾" | hardwood or pine |

key hooks. Wipe up any excess glue with a damp rag, especially between the letters.

When the glue has set, give your key rack a coat of polyurethane varnish or a wipe-on finish and let it dry. Then attach the chain with two number 4, ¾-inch-long brass pan-head screws. Screw in the cup hooks, and your key rack is ready for duty.

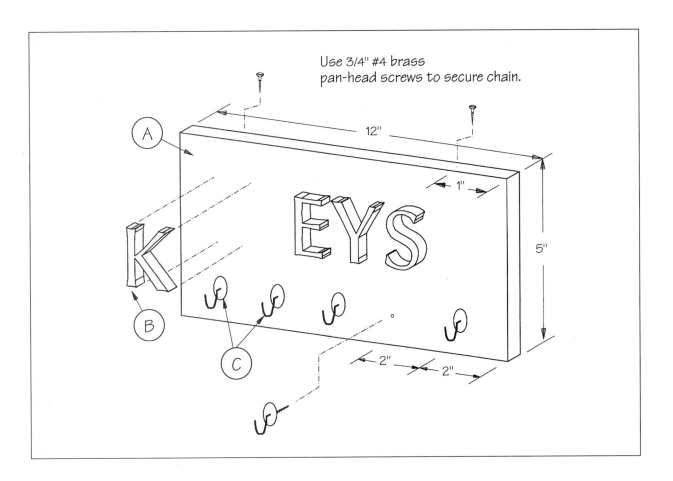

Use 3/4" #4 brass
pan-head screws to secure chain.

# TOY CRATE

Although it looks like a shipping crate, our easy-to-cut-and-assemble toy crate is made to keep a kid's stuff all in one place. Whether it stores sporting gear, a doll and all her accessories, or a hodge-podge of toys, our crate solves the keeping-it-all-together problem.

We used slats made of pine lattice for the sides and 2×2 pine to reinforce corners. You can stencil the crate with your name or your team member's to personalize it.

Begin by measuring the long slats (A), following the dimensions on the Cutting List. With thirteen pieces to cut, both partners can take turns sawing. The short slats (B) are cut next; notice that these pieces are 1/2 inch shorter than the A pieces. The corner posts (C) are cut from 2×2 stock, as are the bottom rails (D).

When all cutting is finished, begin assembly. Use number 4 box nails, and glue and nail a short slat to one of the bottom rails. Make sure the pieces are flush at both ends and along the bottom.

Place one of the corner posts (C) in position so that it butts on top of the bottom rail and is aligned with its end. Place a little glue where the slat meets the corner post, and then nail them together. Do the same at the other end of the rail.

Next, glue and nail a slat to the top of one of the corner posts. Align it, and before

TIME REQUIRED

Four hours for cutting, building, and assembling, plus drying time for glue and finish.

SHOPPING LIST

| Item | Quantity |
|------|----------|
| 3$1/2''$ pine lattice | 40' |
| 2×2 pine furring | 9' |
| carpenter's wood glue | small bottle |
| number 4 box nails | 1 box |
| 120-grit sandpaper | 2 sheets |
| polyurethane varnish | 1 quart |

CUTTING LIST

| Part | Name | Quantity | Size | Material |
|------|------|----------|------|----------|
| A | Long slats | 13 | $1/4'' \times 31/2'' \times 20''$ | pine lattice |
| B | Short slats | 8 | $1/4'' \times 31/2'' \times 191/2''$ | pine lattice |
| C | Corner posts | 4 | $11/2'' \times 11/2'' \times 143/4''$ | pine |
| D | Rails | 2 | $11/2'' \times 11/2'' \times 191/2''$ | pine |

you drive in a second nail, check that the end is square. Then glue and nail the center two slats in place.

Assemble the other end in the same manner. Next, place the two end sections on their sides opposite one another. Apply glue to the end of a long slat, and nail it in place flush with the bottom and square with the end. Do the same at the other end. Glue and nail on the top slat next, and check the crate for squareness. Put in the center two slats, then turn the crate over and glue and nail on the other side.

The bottom slats go on next. Turn your crate over so that the bottom rails are exposed. All the bottom slats are nailed to the bottom rails. Attach the outside slats first. Evenly space the remaining slats, then glue and nail in position.

Your crate is now ready to finish. An easy-to-apply finish of spray varnish or sealer will protect the wood. The final touch is personalizing the crate. Make a stencil by tracing inexpensive block letters, available at any stationery or craft-supply store, onto lightweight cardboard. The older team member should act as surgeon when carefully cutting out the letters, because razor knives are sharp.

Place paper around the stencil to protect the crate from overspray. Decide how you want your letters spaced, and then tape the stencil in place. Use spray paint, and shoot it through the stencil to create your name.

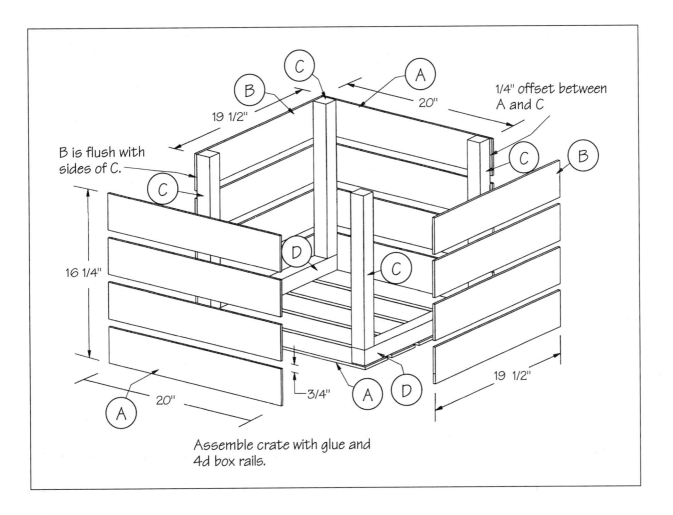

C

B

19 1/2"

A

20"

1/4" offset between
A and C

B is flush with
sides of C.

C

C

B

16 1/4"

D

C

A

20"

3/4"

A

D

19 1/2"

Assemble crate with glue and
4d box rails.

# POSTER CLOCK

Can you find the clock with Mickey and his gang? (Hint: Look at the popcorn!) We gave our favorite characters a timepiece—a quartz clock movement, that is. This poster-clock project requires almost a whole day to create, but the result is well worth it. We had our poster mounted onto a heavy board at a picture-framing store, which cost under $10. Purchasing the wallpaper sizing, cellulose paste, and heavy board would cost about the same. If you have those supplies on hand, however, you might want to mount the poster yourself.

With our poster on the board, we used 1 3/4-inch-wide lattice and parting stop to construct a deep frame to house an inexpensive quartz clock movement. The tiny hour dots are paper stickons that we found at a stationery store.

The frame is constructed first. Begin by laying out the sides (A) and top and bottom pieces (B) on the pine lattice. Then lay out the side and top and bottom stops (C and D) on parting stop. See the Cutting List for all lengths. An inexpensive miter box will guide the apprentice when cutting these parts to length. Square ends are important for good-looking corner joints.

TIME REQUIRED

Eight hours for cutting, building, and assembling, plus drying time for glue and finish.

SHOPPING LIST

| Item | Quantity |
|---|---|
| 1$^{3/4}$″ pine lattice | 12′ |
| $^{1/2}$″ × $^{3/4}$″ parting stop | 12′ |
| 24″ × 36″ mounted poster | 1 |
| carpenter's wood glue | small bottle |
| 120-grit sandpaper | 2 sheets |
| paint, stain, or other finish | 1 pint |
| quartz clock movement | 1 (short shaft) |
| clock hands | 2 |
| stick-on dots | 1 package |
| large picture-hanging bracket | 2 |

CUTTING LIST

| Part | Name | Quantity | Size | Material |
|---|---|---|---|---|
| A | Sides | 2 | 1$^{3/4}$″ × 35″ × $^{1/4}$″ | pine lattice |
| B | Top and bottom | 2 | 1$^{3/4}$″ × 23$^{1/2}$″ × $^{1/4}$″ | pine lattice |
| C | Side stops | 2 | $^{3/4}$″ × 33$^{1/2}$″ × $^{1/2}$″ | pine parting stop |
| D | Top and bottom | 2 | $^{3/4}$″ × 23″ × $^{1/2}$″ | pine parting stop |

Parts C and D are glued to the side and top and bottom pieces (A and B). First, drive small finishing nails into the $^{1/2}$-inch sides of C and D, and then apply glue to the edge of C. Place a scrap of parting stop with its $^{3/4}$-inch side flat on top of A and aligned with its end. This piece acts as a spacer to position part C $^{3/4}$ inch from the end of A. One team member should hold the spacer in place while the other nails part C in place. Assemble the other side of the frame in the same manner.

The top and bottom parts are glued to D using a piece of $^{1/4}$-inch lattice as a spacer. Place the lattice on edge, even with the end of B. Glue and nail parting stop D in place $^{1/4}$ inch from the end and even with the front of B.

The sides, top, and bottom are glued together next. Coat all mating surfaces of the corners with glue. Nail the frame together with small finishing nails driven through side A into the end of D. Place a nail as far from the edge of A as possible to prevent its end from splitting.

String about a dozen rubber bands (depending on size) together to form a temporary clamp. Place the frame face down on a flat surface, and loop the rubber bands around it. Pull the ends tight and loop them over scrap wood, then twist the piece to hold the rubber bands together. Set the frame aside until the glue is dry.

We chose to place our clock in the top left-hand corner. Depending on the poster you choose and where you position the clock, you can vary the diameter of the clock face to suit your design.

Use a compass to lay out the clock face template. It's easy to mark the hour positions

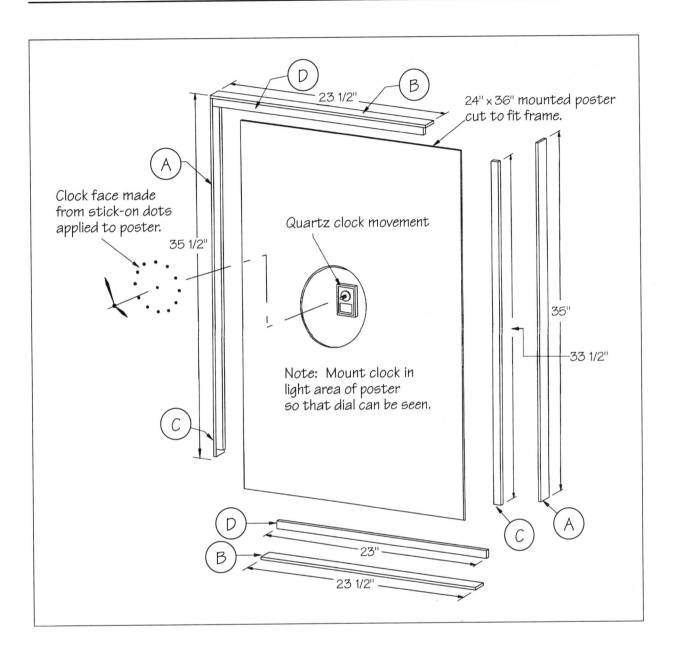

Clock face made from stick-on dots applied to poster.

35 1/2"

Quartz clock movement

Note: Mount clock in light area of poster so that dial can be seen.

23 1/2"

24" x 36" mounted poster cut to fit frame.

35"

33 1/2"

23"

23 1/2"

on the circle if you first divide the circle into quarters, just as if you're cutting a pie. Next, put the compass point at the 3:00 position and set it to the radius of the circle. Swing it until the pencil intersects the circle arc, and mark this point. Then swing your compass in the opposite direction, and mark the other intersection. These points are the 1:00 and 5:00 points. Do this from the 6:00, 9:00, and 12:00 positions, and all hour positions will be accurately marked on the circle arc.

Cut out your clock template and place it on the poster. Mark the center of the clock face on your poster by pushing the compass point through the small hole in the center of the paper template. Remove it, and drill a 5/8-inch hole through cardboard for the clockworks' shaft.

Replace the template, and use it as a guide when placing the self-adhesive dots or numbers on the poster face.

Screw the clockworks' shaft through the

hole, and then thread on the locking nut. The hour hand slips on the shaft, and the minute hand fits over the smaller keyed shaft in the center. Turn the time by adjusting the knob on the back of the clockworks until the minute hand points directly at the twelve. Then adjust the hour hand (it has a press fit and will move around the clock shaft) to point to any hour.

An acorn dress nut is supplied by the clock manufacturer. Thread it on carefully, and do not overtighten.

All that's left to do to get the clock working is to place a AA battery in the clockworks and set the time.

Attach your poster clock to a wall with plastic wall anchors. We used large picture-hanging brackets and finishing nails driven into the lath of a plaster wall. If your walls are made of drywall, use plastic wall anchors. Tighten the anchor screws until their heads are 1/8 inch from the wall surface, then hook the picture brackets over the screw heads.

# MODEL BUILDING BOARD

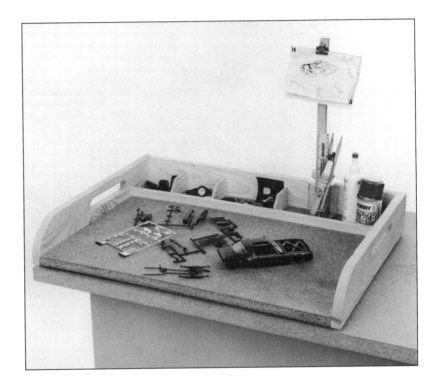

Here's our solution to the two problems all model builders face—where to work and how to keep all the parts neat and organized. This model building board can be placed on top of a desk, kitchen table, or any well-lighted surface to protect your furniture from a young modeler's glue or paint.

The board is portable, with handles for easy carrying. The sturdy base rests on mar-proof feet. Along the back of the board are four compartments, handy for organizing parts and supplies, and an instruction holder with a metal clip that you can purchase at most stationery stores.

This board is easy to construct and has a tough particle board base. We found 3/4-inch-thick, 12-inch-wide shelving at our home center and based the design around it. Purchase 2 feet of this material for a ready-made base. If your lumberyard does not stock shelving that wide, have them cut the base from a quarter sheet of particle board.

Since the back (B) and sides (C) are made from 1×4 pine stock, only their length needs to be measured (see Cutting List). Lay this out, and then cut the sides and back.

Both sides have a 3 1/2-inch-radius rounded end. Use a compass to scribe the arc. Then clamp the side to a table, and cut the rounded corner with a coping saw.

The handle slots are laid out by marking the location of the slot end holes. On

TIME REQUIRED

Four hours for cutting, building, and assembling, plus drying time for glue and finish.

SHOPPING LIST

| Item | Quantity |
|---|---|
| 3/4" flakeboard | 18" × 24" |
| 1×4 pine | 6' |
| 1/2" × 3/4" parting stop | 36" |
| 1 3/4" lattice | 9" |
| number 4 finishing nails | small box |
| number 6, 1" wood screw | 2 |
| 120-grit sandpaper | 2 sheets |
| furniture feet | 4 |
| carpenter's wood glue | small bottle |
| small spring clip | 1 |
| paint, stain, or other finish | 1 pint |

CUTTING LIST

| Part | Name | Quantity | Size | Material |
|---|---|---|---|---|
| A | Bottom | 1 | 24" × 18" × 3/4" | flakeboard |
| B | Back | 1 | 24" × 3 1/2" × 3/4" | pine |
| C | Sides | 2 | 18 3/4" × 3 1/2" × 3/4" | pine |
| D | Compartment front | 1 | 24" × 3/4" × 1/2" | pine parting stop |
| E | Compartment sides | 3 | 3" × 1 3/4" × 1/4" | pine lattice |
| F | Instruction holder | 1 | 12" × 3/4" × 1/2" | pine parting stop |

each side piece (C), make a mark 5 1/2 inches from the square end and 1 1/4 inches from the top edge, and another mark 8 1/2 inches from the rounded end and 1 1/4 inches from the top. Then, for each side piece, secure it to the table and drill a 1-inch hole through each mark.

Connect the two outside edges of these end holes with straight lines. Then use a keyhole or coping saw to cut from hole to hole, creating the handle slot.

Sand the back and sides to remove any rough corners. Wrap sandpaper around a short piece of scrap wood or dowel when sanding the inside of the handle slots.

Your board is ready for assembly. Drive number 3 finishing nails 3 inches apart partway through the sides and back about 1/2 inch from the bottom. Run a bead of glue along the back edge of the bottom. Place the back piece in position, lining it up flush and even with the ends of the bottom. Have one team member hold the bottom in position while the other drives in the nails.

The sides are glued and nailed in place the same way. Put glue on the sides of the bottom piece and the ends of the back. Align the sides with the front edge of the bottom and nail them into place. Then drive three evenly spaced nails into the back edge of the sides to hold them tight against the back of the board.

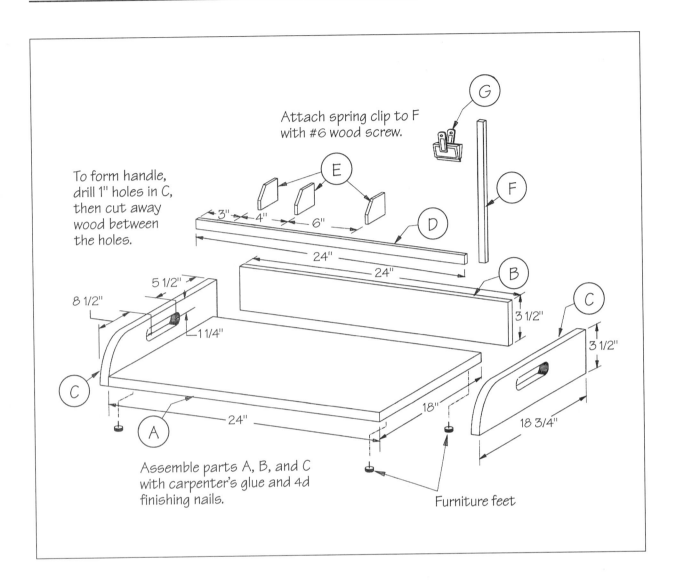

To form handle, drill 1" holes in C, then cut away wood between the holes.

Attach spring clip to F with #6 wood screw.

Assemble parts A, B, and C with carpenter's glue and 4d finishing nails.

Furniture feet

Set the board aside to allow the glue to dry while you cut the compartments. The compartment front (D) is cut from 1/2-by-3/4-inch parting stop, and the dividers from 1/4-by-1 3/4-inch lattice. Following the lengths on the Cutting List, cut part D and also cut out the full-size template for the sides (E). Trace the template for the sides on the lattice, and cut out the remaining three pieces.

Place a compartment divider temporarily in each back corner, against the sides of the model board, to hold the compartment front in place while you glue and nail it with several evenly spaced number 3 nails. Then

put glue on the front and back edges of the compartment pieces, and space them to form three compartments—one 3 inches wide, one 4 inches wide, and one 6 inches wide.

Cut a 12-inch piece of parting stop for the instruction holder (F), and attach the spring clip (G) to one end with a number 6 wood screw. At the other end of the holder, drill a 3/16-inch hole 1 inch from the end. Place the instruction holder in position on the back of the board and make a pencil mark through the hole on the backboard. Drill a 1/16-inch pilot hole through this mark, and mount the instruction holder with a number 6, 1-inch wood screw. Attach one furniture foot to the bottom of each corner.

Your model building board is ready for finishing. A coat of varnish will protect the wood. Give the bottom a single coat to seal it; more finishing will lift if modeling cement is spilled on it. The flakeboard is tough and will stand up to cutting. When the surface becomes coated with globs of glue and paint, scrape it with a razor, give it a light sanding, and recoat with finish.

# BULLETIN BOARD

Who couldn't use this handsome bulletin board? Whether it's a gift for someone's office, kitchen, or bedroom or for the builder's own room, this customized bulletin board will be put to instant use.

The board is simple to construct because basically you are just building a frame around a corkboard. We used a precut 2-by-3-foot cork panel, with corner molding for the frame; both are available at home centers. You can personalize the board by adding a name or initials with letters available at a craft shop.

The sides (A) and top and bottom (B) are cut first. The measurements on the Cutting List are from one point of the 45-degree miter cut to the other. To assure accuracy, mark the length of each individual side (A) and top and bottom (B) on the molding stock and then cut it to length before you mark the next part. Laying out and cutting the parts in this way allows for the thickness of the saw blade. Use your miter box to assure a nice square cut.

To mark the miter cuts, put parts A and B into the miter box so that each side of the molding rests against the bottom of the miter box and the fence. Carefully align the end of the part with the 45-degree slot at the right end of the miter box. Position the

wood so the saw will cut away just enough wood to form the miter but not shorten the part. Then without turning the part, slide it through the miter box until the square end is aligned with the 45-degree slot on the left

Four hours for cutting, building, and assembling, plus drying time for glue and finish.

SHOPPING LIST

| Item | Quantity |
| --- | --- |
| 3/4″ outside corner molding | 12′ |
| Homosote cork panel | 24″ × 36″ |
| construction adhesive | 1 tube |
| 4″ precut letters | as needed |
| carpenter's wood glue | small bottle |
| picture-hanging brackets | 2 |
| number 6, 3/4″ screws | 2 |
| 120-grit sandpaper | 2 sheets |
| paint, stain, or other finish | 1 pint |

CUTTING LIST

| Part | Name | Quantity | Size | Material |
| --- | --- | --- | --- | --- |
| A | Sides (frame) | 2 | 3/4″ × 3/4″ × 361/2″ | outside corner molding |
| B | Top and bottom (frame) | 2 | 3/4″ × 3/4″ × 241/2″ | outside corner molding |
| C | Cork panel | 1 | 1/2″ × 24″ × 36″ | corkboard |
| D | Back support | 1 | 1″ × 24″ × 11/4″ | lattice |

end of the miter box. Then cut the miters of the remaining parts A and B.

Parts A and B are glued to the board with construction adhesive. Run a bead of adhesive down the V of the molding. Be careful not to get adhesive on the lip that will touch the cork; any adhesive on the lip will squeeze out onto the cork front of your bulletin board. Put wood glue on the miter joints, and place the sides, top, and bottom in position.

Tie several rubber bands together to make a temporary clamp. Place the bulletin board face down on a flat surface, and press the frame firmly in place. Stretch the rubber bands around the frame, and loop their ends over a piece of scrap wood. Double-check the alignment of the frame, and set it aside to dry.

Cut the 1-inch lattice to length to make the back support (D) and then glue it to the back of the bulletin board flush with the top molding. This part provides a secure attachment point for the mounting brackets. Then attach the picture-hanging brackets to the back support with number 6, 3/4-inch screws.

You can personalize the bulletin board by gluing on wood letters. Apply the same finish you're using for the frame to the fronts of the letters before you glue them in place. When the finish has dried, put a small amount of adhesive on the backs of the letters and align them. A short name can be run across the top; for a longer name, use smaller letters and run them down one side of the board.

After the glue has dried, sand the frame

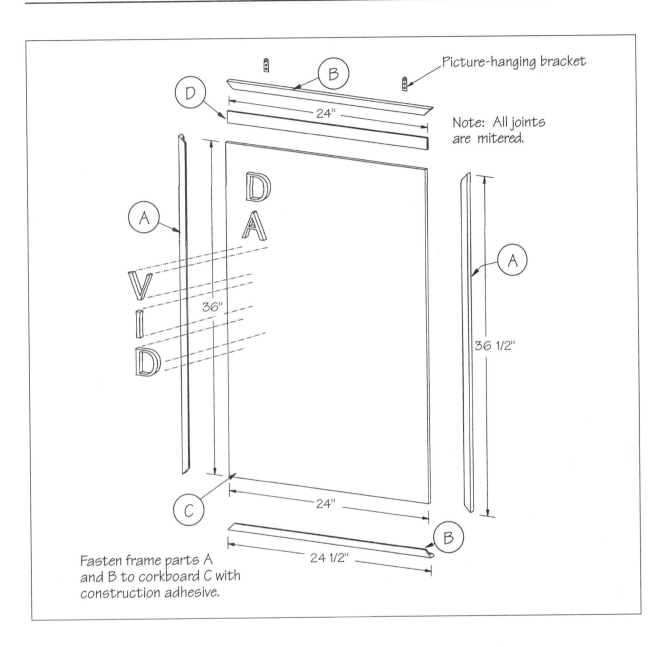

Picture-hanging bracket

B

D

24"

Note: All joints are mitered.

A

D
A
V
I
D

36"

A

36 1/2"

24"

C

B

Fasten frame parts A and B to corkboard C with construction adhesive.

24 1/2"

with 120-grit sandpaper. We used a wipe-on finish to seal the frame, but you can also use paint. Be careful when applying finish around the cork. To keep the finish from getting on the cork, place a piece of cardboard tight against the frame to shield the face.

# ELECTRONIC GAME CARTRIDGE HOLDER

Have Nintendo and Genesis invaded your house? Keeping electronic game cartridges safe and organized can become a problem as their numbers multiply. Here is an easy-to-make modular game cartridge holder that will keep everything shipshape.

Our cartridge cube holds eight games and is made of pine with a natural finish. You can construct several and stack them together to hold your expanding game library.

Construction is easy, although there are many small parts to cut. Use a miter box to ensure square ends. Following the lengths on the Cutting List, cut the two sides and center partition (A), the top and bottom (B), and the three back parts (C and D) to size, but do not cut (D) to width now.

The supports (E) are cut from parting stop. Since a dozen are needed, make a gauge by clamping a piece of scrap to the table. Adjust the position of the miter box so that the distance from the cutoff slot and the stop gauge is 3 1/2 inches. Then all you have to do is push the parting stop through the miter box until it hits the stop block and cut. Repeat for each piece, and all the supports will be the same length without your having to measure each one individually. Take turns cutting. While one cuts, the other can sand the support pieces smooth with 120-grit sandpaper.

TIME REQUIRED

Four hours for cutting, building, and assembling, plus drying time for glue and finish.

SHOPPING LIST

| Item | Quantity |
|---|---|
| 1×4 pine | 4' |
| $3^{1}/_{2}''$ pine lattice | 6' |
| $1/_{2}'' \times 3/_{4}''$ parting stop | 5' |
| $7/_{8}''$ wire brads | small box |
| carpenter's wood glue | small bottle |
| 120-grit sandpaper | 2 sheets |
| paint, stain, or other finish | 1 pint |

CUTTING LIST

| Part | Name | Quantity | Size | Material |
|---|---|---|---|---|
| A | Sides and partition | 3 | $3/_{4}'' \times 3^{1}/_{2}'' \times 8^{1}/_{2}''$ | pine |
| B | Top and bottom | 2 | $1/_{4}'' \times 3^{1}/_{2}'' \times 11^{1}/_{4}''$ | pine lattice |
| C | Large back pieces | 2 | $1/_{4}'' \times 3^{1}/_{2}'' \times 11^{1}/_{4}''$ | pine lattice |
| D | Small back piece | 1 | $1/_{4}'' \times 2'' \times 11^{1}/_{4}''$ | pine lattice |
| E | Supports | 12 | $1/_{2}'' \times 3/_{4}'' \times 3^{1}/_{2}''$ | pine parting stop |

Use a square to mark the location of the supports on the two side pieces. On each, draw three layout lines $2^{1}/_{4}$ inches apart, with the first line $2^{1}/_{4}$ inches up from the bottom. Do the same on both sides of the center partition.

The supports are glued and nailed into place using $7/_{8}$-inch wire brads. First, align the top edges of the supports on the layout lines. Make sure the supports are flush with the front and back edges of the partition and sides. Install the supports from the bottom up. Before you secure them in place, check that the supports on the sides are aligned with those on the partition when facing toward one another.

The top and bottom are put on next. Glue and nail the side pieces flush with the ends of the top and bottom, and then place the center partition in position. After installing the center partition, turn the cube so that the best-looking edges of this assembly are facing down, and nail and glue on the two larger back parts (C), starting at the bottom of the cube. Put the third back piece (D) in place and mark the needed width by running a pencil line along the top of the cube. Cut the piece to size, and then nail and glue it into place.

Sand your cube with 120-grit sandpaper. If an end or back piece extends slightly beyond the sides, place a piece of sandpaper on a flat surface, and push the cube back and forth over the paper. Your cube sides will then be smooth and square.

We finished our cube with a transparent wipe-on sealer. You might want to paint yours a bright color.

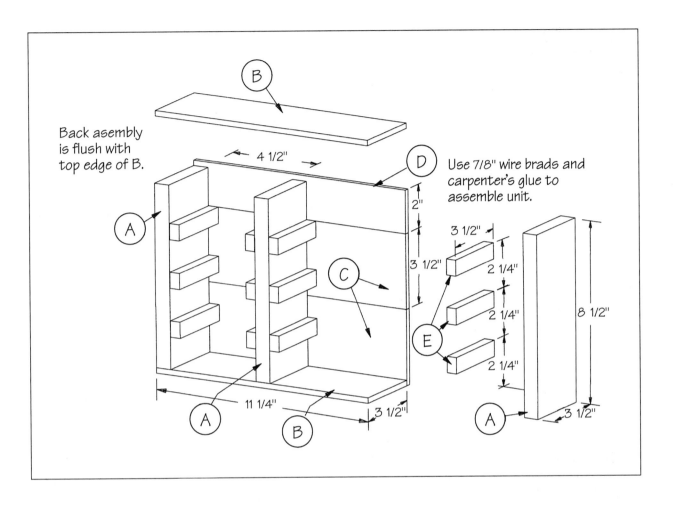

Back asembly
is flush with
top edge of B.

4 1/2"

D

Use 7/8" wire brads and
carpenter's glue to
assemble unit.

A

2"

3 1/2"

C

3 1/2"

2 1/4"

2 1/4"

E

2 1/4"

8 1/2"

11 1/4"

A

B

3 1/2"

A

3 1/2"

# HOME COMPUTER STAND

This nifty shelf raises up a computer screen so it's more clearly visible, while at the same time providing more desk space. A handy compartment on one side is for storing a mouse and its pad, and the larger compartment is for the keyboard. We made ours for a leftie, but you can make yours for right-hand use simply by reversing the placement of the divider.

The shelf is easy to build because it is designed around dimensional 1×12 and 1×8 lumber. All you have to do is cut the pieces to length and then glue and nail them together. This lumber can be pretty rough and will need a light sanding before you apply a rub-on finish.

Five saw cuts are all that's needed to form the parts of the stand. Cut the top (D) from the 1×12 piece of lumber. The back (B), ends (A), and partition (C) are all cut from the 1×8 stock. Lay out the length of each

piece individually and cut it to length before you cut the next. This will guarantee that each part is the proper length.

Assembly could not be easier. Draw a pencil line 3/8 inch from the back edge of each end piece (A) to help you in positioning the nails. Then drive five evenly spaced number 4 finishing nails along these lines, just deep enough that their points begin to

TIME REQUIRED

Two to three hours for cutting, building, and assembling, plus drying time for glue and finish.

SHOPPING LIST

| Item | Quantity |
|---|---|
| 1×12 pine | 3' |
| 1×8 pine | 6' |
| carpenter's wood glue | small bottle |
| number 4 finishing nails | small box |
| 120-grit sandpaper | 2 sheets |
| paint, stain, or other finish | 1 pint |

CUTTING LIST

| Part | Name | Quantity | Size | Material |
|---|---|---|---|---|
| A | Ends | 2 | $3/4'' \times 7 1/4'' \times 11 1/4''$ | pine |
| B | Back | 1 | $3/4'' \times 7 1/4'' \times 30 1/2''$ | pine |
| C | Partition | 1 | $3/4'' \times 7 1/4'' \times 10 1/2''$ | pine |
| D | Top | 1 | $3/4'' \times 11 1/4'' \times 32''$ | pine |

come out the other side of the board. Apply glue to one end of the back (B), align one end piece flush with the back edge, and nail it in place. Apply glue to the other end of the back and install the remaining end piece the same way.

The partition (C) can be located just about anyplace along the back. In fact, you can make several; just be sure to allow enough room to slide the keyboard under the top. We located the partition 8 inches from one end.

Turn the assembly over so it is resting facedown on the ends with the back up. Then draw a pencil layout line down the back 8 3/4 inches from one end to help align the nails. Drive five evenly spaced finishing nails along this line as you did with the ends. Apply glue to the end of the partition, lift up

the unit, and put the partition in place under the back. Drive the nails through the back into the edge of the partition.

Next, turn the unit over and install the top. Apply glue to the top edge of the sides and back, and then place the top in position. Check the alignment at the ends and back, then drive nails through the top into the ends and back. Be careful to keep the nails within 3/8 inch of the top's edge to avoid splitting the wood below.

Before the glue has time to set up, use a damp rag to remove any excess that may have squeezed out of the joints. Then give the unit a careful sanding. Pay special attention to getting the end grain smooth so that your stand will take stain evenly. You can skip the staining if you like the look of natural pine.

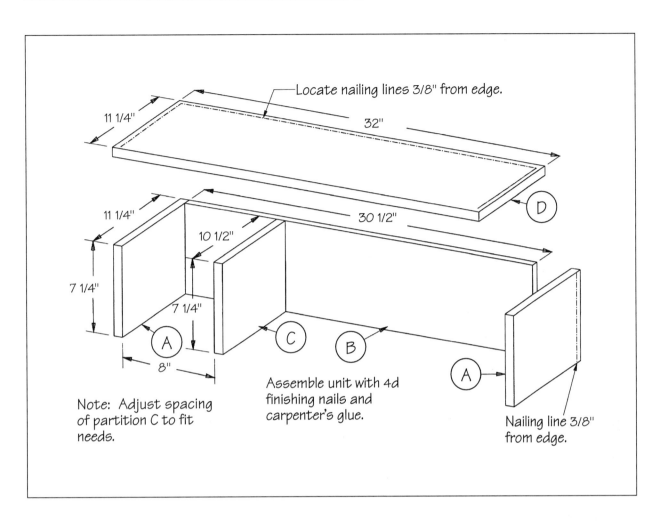

Locate nailing lines 3/8" from edge.

11 1/4"

32"

11 1/4"

30 1/2"

10 1/2"

D

7 1/4"

7 1/4"

A

C

B

A

8"

Note: Adjust spacing of partition C to fit needs.

Assemble unit with 4d finishing nails and carpenter's glue.

Nailing line 3/8" from edge.

# BOOK RACK

A cribbage board inspired our design for this nifty little desktop book rack. Instead of pegs being used to keep score, these pegs hold a movable partition in place.

We used 1×8 pine lumber, but oak or any other hardwood will make an even more handsome book rack. Like craftsmen of past generations, you'll make your own doweling jig to help you drill holes for the base and partition pegs. This jig aligns the peg holes in the movable partition and base. The sides of the rack can be strengthened with the addition of glue blocks under the bottom piece.

All the parts are cut from one 1×8 pine board. Lay out the measurements for the ends (A), bottom (B), and movable partition (C) on the pine, following the Cutting List. Cut these pieces out, then cut the jig from scrap wood.

Next, lay out the guide holes on the jig. Use a tape measure and pencil to make marks along its length 1 1/4 inches from each end and in the center 3 5/8 inches from each end. Use a combination square to draw straight lines through these marks across the width of the jig. Find the center of the jig ends by measuring 1 1/2 inches from each side, and make a mark at each end. Use the square to draw a straight line through this mark down the center of the jig. This forms three Xs, which mark the location of the guide holes. Use a drill with a 3/8-inch bit to

TIME REQUIRED

Six hours for cutting, building, and assembling, plus
drying time for glue and
finish.

SHOPPING LIST

| Item | Quantity |
|---|---|
| 1×8 clear pine | 5′ |
| 3/8″ hardwood dowel | 1′ |
| number 6 finishing nails | small box |
| carpenter's wood glue | small bottle |
| 120-grit sandpaper | 2 sheets |
| paint, stain, or other finish | 1 pint |

CUTTING LIST

| Part | Name | Quantity | Size | Material |
|---|---|---|---|---|
| A | Ends | 2 | $3/4″ \times 7^{1/4}″ \times 9″$ | pine |
| B | Bottom | 1 | $3/4″ \times 7^{1/4}″ \times 14″$ | pine |
| C | Partition | 1 | $3/4″ \times 7^{1/4}″ \times 4″$ | pine |
| D | Dowels | 3 | $3/8″ \times 1^{1/4}″$ | hardwood dowel |
| E | Jig | 1 | $3/4″ \times 7^{1/4}″ \times 3″$ | pine scrap |

bore these holes. One team member should
check that the drill is held square to the jig
to make sure the holes are straight.

Now mark the location of the peg holes
on the edge of the bottom of the rack (B).
Measure 4 inches from one end, then use
your square to draw a straight line across
the bottom. Repeat with the other end, and
then mark off and draw lines at 2-inch
intervals between these two lines.

Now you are ready to drill peg holes in
the bottom. Align the holes of the jig with
one of the layout lines, and clamp the jig to
the bottom piece. Check that the end of the
jig is flush with the sides of the bottom,
then drill three 3/8-inch holes through the
bottom, using the holes in the jig as your
guide.

Remove the jig, align the holes over
another layout line, clamp it to the bottom,
and repeat the drilling. Carefully check the
jig alignment before each drilling, and your
movable partition pegs will fit exactly.

After you have drilled all twelve peg
holes in the bottom, nail your jig to a piece
of scrap with number 6 finishing nails to
form a doweling guide. Align the scrap piece
so that the jig holes will be centered along
the bottom of the movable partition (C).
When your doweling jig is complete, position it on the bottom edge of the partition so
that its end is flush with the side of the partition. Clamp the jig into place, then drill
3/8-inch holes, 1 inch deep, in the bottom
edge of the partition, using the jig to guide
you. Have one team member check that the
drill is held straight.

Remove your jig, and put a drop of glue
on the end of a 1¹/4–inch length of 3/8-inch
dowel. Tap it into a hole in the partition.
Glue the other pieces of dowel in place the
same way.

The ends are held to the bottom with
four number 6 finishing nails and glue. Lay
out the position of the nails by measuring
up 1¹/8 inches from the bottom of each end

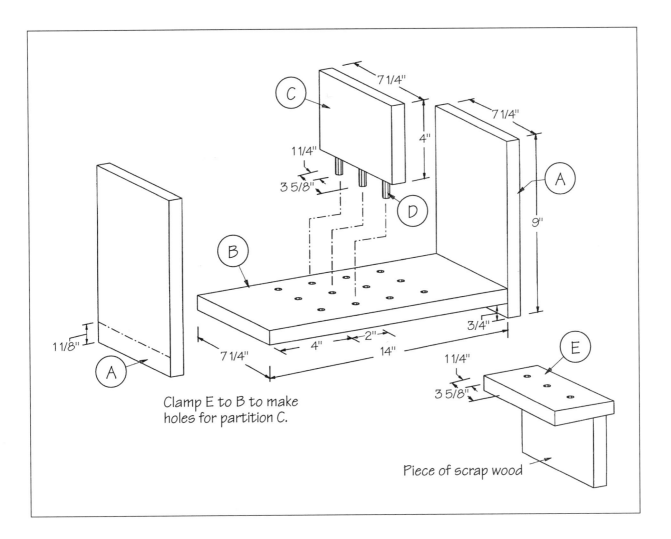

7 1/4"

C

7 1/4"

4"

1 1/4"

3 5/8"

D

A

9"

B

3/4"

1 1/8"

4"

2"

A

7 1/4"

14"

1 1/4"

E

3 5/8"

Clamp E to B to make
holes for partition C.

Piece of scrap wood

and using the square to draw a straight line across each. On the inner sides of the ends, draw another line 3/4 inch from the bottom to help you align the ends with the bottom when you attach them. Then drive four evenly spaced number 6 finishing nails along each of the first two lines you drew. Pound these nails into the wood just deep enough so that their points emerge from the other side.

Put glue on one end of the bottom (B), and place one end piece (A) in position so that the nails are centered along the edge of piece B. Use the layout lines you drew 3/4

inch from the bottom on the inner side of each end as a guide. Have one team member hold the pieces in position while the other drives the nails. Then glue and nail up the other side. Use a nail set to sink the nail heads below the surface of the wood.

Sand all corners smooth with 120-grit sandpaper. If the partition pegs fit too tightly in the base, work your drill with the 3/8-inch bit back and forth in the holes to enlarge them.

Our book rack is finished with a light-colored stain. We also gave it a coat of paste wax for long-lasting protection.

# COLLECTOR'S BRIEFCASE

A prized collection of minia-ture cars, ceramic horses, or any other treasured items can be protected and show-cased in our briefcase. We used a piece of inexpensive acrylic window pane for the sides so you can see your col-lectibles from all angles.

Although small, this proj-ect requires considerable time, as many small pieces must be cut and assembled. But your time will be well spent, because you'll have created a lasting showcase for any important collection. And the case is portable so that it can be carried around to show the collection to friends.

We sized the briefcase for Hot Wheels or Matchbox cars, but you can change the size of the spacers, adjusting the height of shelves to accommodate just about any small collectible item. You can also cut more spacers and position them to make individ-ual compartments for each treasure.

Cutting spacers and trim pieces will take as much time as the actual assembly. Begin by cutting the 1×4 pine stock into two 14-inch-long pieces for the top (A) and bot-tom (B). Then lay out a 2-inch width on the piece that will be used for the bottom, and clamp a straight piece of scrap along this line to help guide your saw as you cut B to width. Repeat the process for A, but cut it 1 3/4 inches wide to allow clearance for the removable acrylic front pane.

The sides (C) are cut from 2-inch-wide lattice. Measure their length according to

TIME REQUIRED

Eight hours for cutting, building, and assembling, plus drying time for glue and finish.

### SHOPPING LIST

| Item | Quantity |
| --- | --- |
| 1×4 pine | 3' |
| 2" lattice | 3' |
| 1" lattice | 10' |
| 1³/₄" lattice | 10' |
| ¹/₈" acrylic window pane | 14" × 20" |
| drawer pull | 1 |
| ⁷/₈" wire brads | small box |
| 120-grit sandpaper | 2 sheets |
| carpenter's wood glue | small bottle |
| paint, stain, or other finish | 1 pint |

### CUTTING LIST

| Part | Name | Quantity | Size | Material |
| --- | --- | --- | --- | --- |
| A | Top | 1 | 3/4" × 1³/₄" × 14" | pine |
| B | Bottom | 1 | 3/4" × 2" × 14" | pine |
| C | Sides | 2 | 1/4" × 2" × 10" | pine lattice |
| D | Shelves | 4 | 1/4" × 1³/₄" × 14" | pine lattice |
| E | Spacers | 8 | 1/4" × 1³/₄" × 1¹/₂" | pine lattice |
| F | Top trim pieces | 2 | 1/4" × 1" × 14¹/₂" | pine lattice |
| G | Side trim pieces | 2 | 1/4" × 1" × 9" | pine lattice |
| H | Bottom trim pieces | 2 | 1/4" × 1" × 12¹/₂" | pine lattice |
| I | Front pane | 1 | 1/8" × 9¹/₄" × 14" | acrylic |
| J | Back pane | 1 | 1/8" × 8¹/₂" × 14" | acrylic |

the Cutting List, and cut them to size using a wood miter box to ensure square cuts. The shelves (D) are cut from lattice 1³/₄ inches wide. Measure them and cut to size, following the Cutting List.

Since there are eight spacers (E) all the same size, use a stop block to help cut the pieces. Place a scrap of wood 1¹/₂ inches from the cutting slot of the miter box, and clamp it to your table or miter box. Then push the 1³/₄-inch lattice down the miter box until it hits, stop, and make your cut. Repeat for all eight spacers. While one car-

penter is cutting, the other can be sanding the parts.

Cut the top trim (F) and side trim (G) to length from 1-inch-wide lattice. Don't cut the bottom trim (H) to length yet.

Your local hardware store will cut acrylic panes (I and J) for you, or you can purchase a standard size pane large enough to cut both from. Acrylic can be scored with a sharp knife and then carefully cracked along the score line.

After all this cutting, the assembly is easy. Put glue on one end of the top (A), and

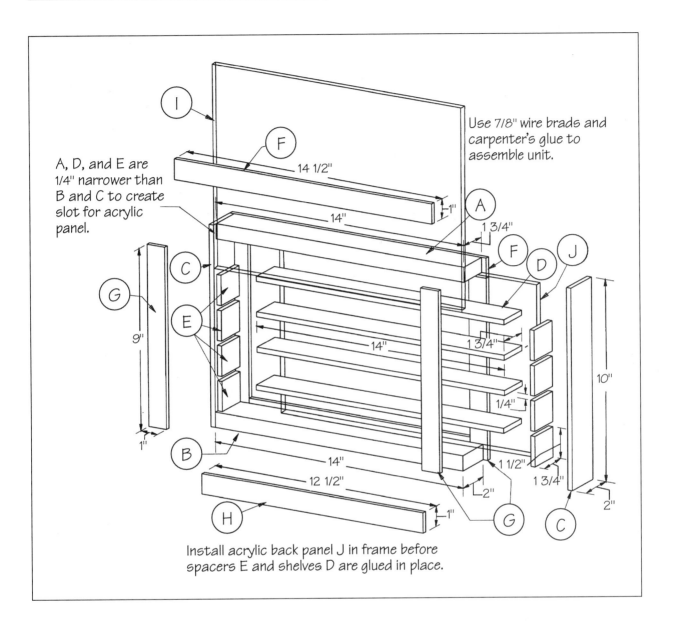

A, D, and E are 1/4" narrower than B and C to create slot for acrylic panel.

Use 7/8" wire brads and carpenter's glue to assemble unit.

14 1/2"

14"

1"

1 3/4"

1 3/4"

1/4"

9"

14"

1"

14"

12 1/2"

1 1/2"

2"

1 3/4"

10"

2"

1"

Install acrylic back panel J in frame before spacers E and shelves D are glued in place.

nail the side (C) flush with the top piece and even with its back. Piece C will extend beyond piece A at the front, because the side piece is wider than the top piece. Use 7/8-inch wire brads, and place them back from the edges of the sides to prevent splitting. Repeat for the bottom (B).

Turn the case over, and glue and nail up the other side. Be sure to align the top and side as you did on the other end, keeping in mind that the top is narrower than the sides.

First glue and nail the top and side trim (F and G) in place with 7/8-inch wire brads on the back of the case. Align the trim pieces flush with the sides and square at the ends. When nailing on the side trim, take care to drive the nails in carefully to avoid splitting the narrow side piece.

Measure the distance between the side trim pieces to get an exact fit for the bottom trim (H). Cut it to this measurement. Nail and glue into place. Then sink all nail heads with a nail set.

Turn the case over, and insert the back pane (J) into the case. Your spacers and shelves go in next. Put a drop of glue on the back of a spacer, and place it snugly against the inside and bottom of the case; place another spacer in the opposite corner. All spacers and shelves are 1/4 inch short of the front edge of the sides to leave room for the sliding front pane.

Put the first shelf in place, pushing it down against the spacers. Glue up two more spacers, and place them tightly against the inside and top of the first shelf to hold it in place. Then insert the next shelf, and repeat for all spacers and shelves. Place a small amount of glue on the ends of the top shelf and push it into place; it doesn't need a spacer above it.

The front trim is glued and nailed into place the same way as the back trim. The top trim is only glued to the front edge of the side, leaving a 1/4-inch gap behind it for the front pane to slide into.

We used a modern-style drawer pull for a handle, but you can choose whatever style suits your taste. Drill holes for your handle according to installation instructions furnished by the manufacturer.

A natural finish of tung oil is used to highlight the pine. If you decide to stain your case, apply sealer to the end grain of the pine, or else those areas will absorb more stain than the sides and turn out much darker.

# BOTTLE RACK

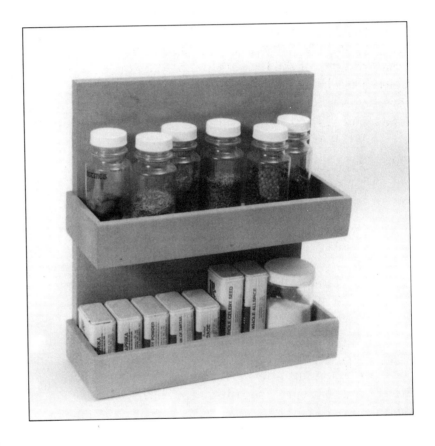

In the kitchen, this rack can be used to organize spice bottles; on the bathroom counter, it can store pills and toiletries. This handy little bottle rack has all kinds of uses around the house. It can either stand alone or be mounted on a wall.

We used scrap flakeboard with lattice sides and painted our bottle rack with two coats of enamel spray paint. Plywood will work just as well, or you can use a piece of 1×12 lumber for the back. Materials for this bottle rack are inexpensive, and it makes a useful and attractive gift.

Cut the shelves (B) from a short piece of 1×4 pine. Then cut the shelf fronts (C) from 1 3/4-inch lattice. Use an inexpensive wood miter box for a clean square cut. Cut the shelf sides (D) from the lattice, too.

Assembly is easy. Measure 6 1/4 inches from the bottom of the back (A), and mark a straight line across its width. This is where you align the bottom edge of the top shelf.

Drive four number 6 finishing nails through the back 3/8 inch above its bottom edge and 3/8 inch above the top shelf layout line.

Put glue on the back edge of the bottom shelf, and have one team member hold it on the edge while the other positions it on the back. The first shelf should be aligned with

TIME REQUIRED

Four hours for cutting, building, and assembling, plus drying time for glue and finish.

SHOPPING LIST

| Item | Quantity |
|---|---|
| flakeboard scrap (at least 12″ × 13″) | 1 |
| 1×4 pine | 2′ |
| 1³/4″ lattice | 5′ |
| number 6 finishing nails | 2 dozen |
| 7/8″ wire brads | small box |
| carpenter's wood glue | small bottle |
| 120-grit sandpaper | 2 sheets |
| paint, stain, or other finish | 12-ounce spray can |

CUTTING LIST

| Part | Name | Quantity | Size | Material |
|---|---|---|---|---|
| A | Back | 1 | 3/4″ × 12″ × 13″ | flakeboard |
| B | Shelves | 2 | 3/4″ × 31/2″ × 12″ | pine |
| C | Shelf fronts | 2 | 1/4″ × 13/4″ × 121/2″ | pine lattice |
| D | Shelf sides | 4 | 1/4″ × 13/4″ × 41/4″ | pine lattice |

the ends of the back and flush with the bottom. Nail it into place.

Glue up the back edge of the top shelf, and align its bottom edge with your layout line. Drive nails into the wood to secure it.

The sides of the shelves (D) go on next. Check that the shelves are square with the back, and then put glue on the shelf ends. Align the sides with the front edge of the shelf, and nail them into place with 7/8-inch brads. Place the brads as far from the edges as possible to avoid splitting the wood.

Now glue and nail on the shelf fronts (C). Align them flush with the ends of the sides, and drive 7/8-inch wire brads through the fronts into the ends of the sides and along the bottom edge into the shelf.

If you used plywood for the back, fill any gaps along the edge with wood putty, then sand your rack smooth with 120-grit sandpaper.

We gave our bottle rack two coats of enamel spray paint and plan to use it as a freestanding shelf. Add a hanging bracket to the back if you want to mount the rack on a wall.

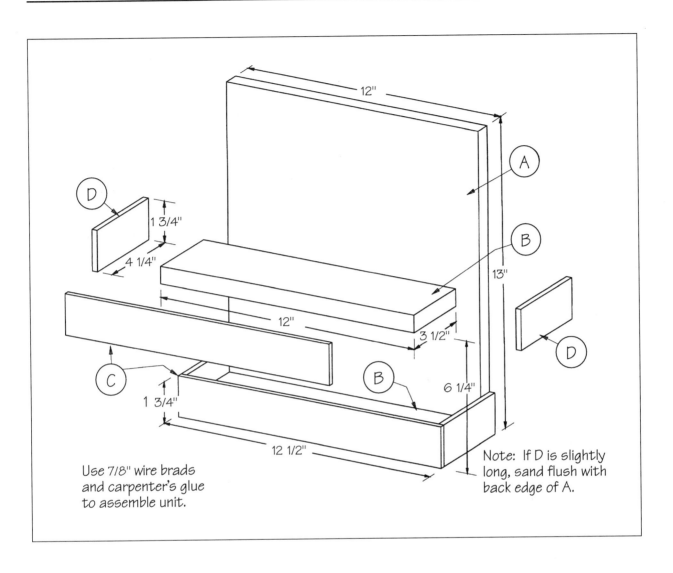

12"

D

1 3/4"

4 1/4"

A

B

13"

12"

3 1/2"

D

B

6 1/4"

C

1 3/4"

12 1/2"

Use 7/8" wire brads
and carpenter's glue
to assemble unit.

Note:  If D is slightly
long, sand flush with
back edge of A.

# PET NEST

Here's a great project to build for your best friend. Our drawerlike pet cradle will become the favorite snoozing spot for your cat or dog. It is made from a single 8-foot 1×6 and scraps of flakeboard and carpeting. The carpeting isn't tacked down so it can be removed or replaced when necessary.

The base of our pet nest is cut from a piece of 18-inch flakeboard shelving. If your pet needs a larger area, have the yardman at your local lumberyard cut a base from a scrap piece of flakeboard to fit your pet, and then increase the length of the sides and front and back.

Construction is fast and easy. Begin by cutting the sides (B) and front and back (C) to size, following the Cutting List. Then lay out the front entrance on C. Use a combination square to draw two sloping 45-degree lines, beginning at a point on the top edge 4 inches from the end. Lay out the bottom of the entrance by drawing a line 2 1/2 inches from the top and parallel to it.

Drill a 3/8 inch-pilot hole at the intersection of the angled lines and the straight lines. If you don't have a 3/8-inch drill, any size hole will do, or you may skip this step and leave the board straight.

Cut out the entrance opening with a saw, then sand the edges of the opening smooth with 120-grit sandpaper wrapped around a small block of wood.

On each of the B and C pieces, drive five evenly spaced number 4 finishing nails 3/8 inch from the bottom. Drive a number 4 finishing nail 3/8 inch from the top corners of

TIME REQUIRED

Four hours for cutting, building, and assembling, plus drying time for glue and finish.

SHOPPING LIST

| Item | Quantity |
|---|---|
| 1×6 pine | 8' |
| 3/4" flakeboard | 18" × 24" |
| carpet scrap | 18" × 24" |
| carpenter's wood glue | small bottle |
| number 4 finishing nails | small box |
| 120-grit sandpaper | 2 sheets |
| 2" vinyl stick-on letters | 1 set |

CUTTING LIST

| Part | Name | Quantity | Size | Material |
|---|---|---|---|---|
| A | Base | 1 | 3/4" × 18" × 24" | flakeboard |
| B | Sides | 2 | 3/4" × 5 1/2" × 18" | pine |
| C | Front and back | 2 | 3/4" × 5 1/2" × 25 1/2" | pine |

the front and back (C) to hold the front and back pieces tightly against the ends of the sides (B).

Assembly is easy. Have one team member hold the base (A) while the other runs glue down one side edge. Place the side (B) flush with the ends of the base (A), and nail

it into place. Install the other side, and then glue and nail on the front and back.

Give your pet nest a sanding with 120-grit sandpaper to round slightly any sharp corner. Then cut a piece of scrap carpet to fit the base. We made our nest a very personal home with pressure-sensitive vinyl letters.

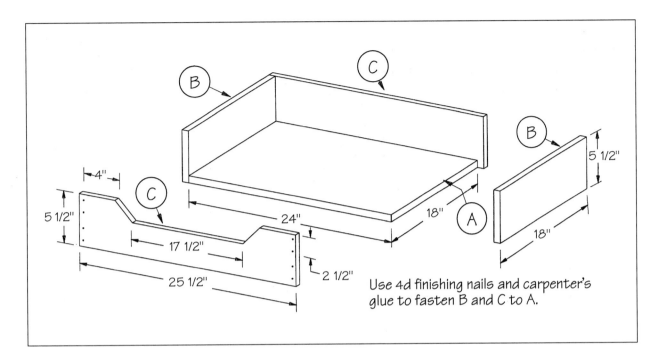

Use 4d finishing nails and carpenter's
glue to fasten B and C to A.

# FOOTSTOOL

$O$ur Shaker-style footstool combines the talents of woodworking and cord weaving. Impressive looking as it is, it is not difficult to make.

The legs are made of inexpensive 2×2 furring lumber, and eight rungs are cut from 7/8-inch dowel stock. We used 6-millimeter macramé cording that came in a 100-yard skein for the seat; you can choose heavy yarn, purse cording, or even heavy twine.

Construction of the stool frame is easy. Following the Cutting List, cut the legs (A) from 2×2 stock and the rungs (B) from 7/8-inch dowel stock.

Next, lay out the holes for the dowels on the legs. Using a combination square, draw a line across the face of the leg 1 inch down from its top. Then draw another line 6 inches down the leg from this line. Mark the center of these lines (3/4 inch from either side) to indicate the center of the rung holes. Lay out the other three legs in the same way.

The lower set of rung holes, located on the adjacent faces, are marked out next. Before you mark these holes, pair up the legs by turning them on their sides so that the upper holes are facing one another. Make an X on each piece on the side facing up. Lay out the location of the lower holes on these sides, and you'll have matching

TIME REQUIRED

Eight hours for cutting, building, and assembling, plus drying time for glue and finish.

SHOPPING LIST

| Item | Quantity |
|---|---|
| 2×2 pine | 6′ |
| 7/8″ dowel | 4 (3′ long) |
| carpenter's wood glue | small bottle |
| 120-grit sandpaper | 2 sheets |
| paint, stain, or other finish | 1 pint |
| yarn, cord, or twine | 100 yards |

CUTTING LIST

| Part | Name | Quantity | Size | Material |
|---|---|---|---|---|
| A | Legs | 4 | 1½″ × 1½″ × 12½″ | pine |
| B | Rungs | 8 | 7/8″ × 13½″ | dowel |

pairs of legs. The lower rung holes at the top are located 2⅛ inches from the top of each leg, and the lower rung holes at the bottom are 6 inches farther down.

Before you drill your holes, recheck that you have matching legs. Place them in position and see that there are matching dowel holes, upper holes opposite upper holes. Then drill a 7/8-inch hole 1 inch deep through each layout mark. Have one member of the team check that the drill remains straight.

Assembly is quick. Apply a small amount of glue to the ends of the dowels, and place them in the holes. Use a hammer and a scrap block of wood to tap the dowels until they reach the bottoms of the holes. Place the stool on a flat surface, and check that all the legs touch the ground. If they don't, twist the stool into correct alignment.

After the glue has dried, sand your stool with 120-grit sandpaper, and give it several coats of tung oil.

Stringing the seat is next. Nine groups of six strands each make up the pattern. Begin by tacking the taped end of the cord-

ing to a leg, just under the lower rung. Then wind fifty-four rows, or "warps," around the lower pair of rungs. When finished, you should have fifty-four strands of yarn above and below the rungs. At the end of the fifty-fourth row, pull out about 4 more feet of cord and then cut it off. Tape one end to a pencil or craft stick, which you'll use as a weaving needle. Now you're ready to begin "wefting" the pattern.

There is a top and bottom pattern. First you weave your cord through the top strands, and then you return it underneath, weaving it through the bottom layer. Pull the stick and cording over the lower rung, loop it around, and then run it under the seat to the nearest upper rung. Count over six strands, and tuck the stick under the seventh. Count five more (six total) and bring the stick up and over the next six, and so on. Continue weaving above and below the groups of six strands until you reach the other side.

You should wind up above the last six strands. Turning the stool over, pull the cording over the high-rung side and over the

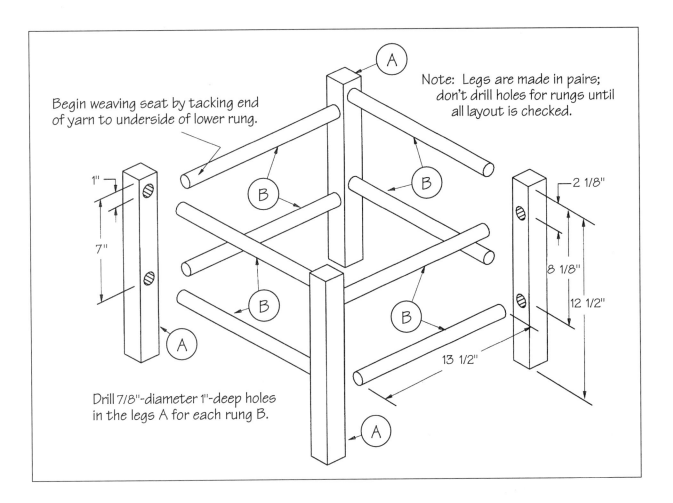

Begin weaving seat by tacking end of yarn to underside of lower rung.

Note: Legs are made in pairs; don't drill holes for rungs until all layout is checked.

1"

7"

A

B

B

B

B

A

A

A

2 1/8"

8 1/8"

12 1/2"

13 1/2"

Drill 7/8"-diameter 1"-deep holes in the legs A for each rung B.

first six strands of cording on the underside of the stool. Continue weaving the cording over and under, alternating every six strands. When you get to the other side, continue the pattern, turning the stool right side up.

After weaving your first six rows, the seventh row is the opposite of them. Run your needle below the next group of six strands, and reverse every six rows until you reach the end.

When you run out of yarn, simply tie the end to another piece of 4-foot-long cording. Plan your splices for the underside of the stool, and tuck the knot inside. Tack the end to a corner dowel when you're through.

# NAPKIN HOLDER

Useful as well as good-looking, our napkin holder is crafted from solid oak. Both master craftsman and apprentice will be challenged by this project. Working with hardwoods is slightly more demanding than working with pine, because all fasteners require pilot holes. Both you and your apprentice should complete another project before attempting this napkin holder.

The holder is made from scrap pieces of oak that you can purchase at your local lumberyard. If they don't have the 1/2-inch-thick stock called for to make the ends, substitute the 3/4-inch-thick stock used for the base. The screw holes are filled with oak plugs; if you can't find them, buy more of the 3/8-inch dowel stock used for the napkin weight, and cut your own plugs.

Begin construction by cutting the base (A) and ends (B) to size, following the Cutting List. Sand the sides of the ends smooth, and round the edges slightly. Sand the base, except for the ends where they will be glued.

Next, lay out the screw holes in the ends. Locate the centers of these 3/8-inch holes 3/8 inch from the bottom edge and 3/4 inch from each side. Use a combination square to draw a line across the ends 3/8 inch from the bottom, then make marks along this line 3/4 inch in from each side. Lay out all four end pieces in the same way.

Two holes are now drilled at each of these points. First, drill a 3/8-inch hole 1/8 inch deep through your layout marks in all

TIME REQUIRED

Eight hours for cutting, building, and assembling, plus drying time for glue and finish.

SHOPPING LIST

| Item | Quantity |
|------|----------|
| 1×8 oak | 2' |
| 1/2″ × 3″ oak | 2' |
| 3/8″ hardwood dowel | 1' |
| 3/8″ oak plugs | 12 |
| number 6, 1″ wood screws (flat headed) | 12 |
| carpenter's wood glue | small bottle |
| 120-grit sandpaper | 2 sheets |
| paint, stain, or other finish | 1 pint |
| sliver of bar soap | 1 |

CUTTING LIST

| Part | Name | Quantity | Size | Material |
|------|------|----------|------|----------|
| A | Base | 1 | 3/4″ × 7″ × 7″ | oak |
| B | Ends | 4 | 1/2″ × 3″ × 51/2″ | oak |
| C | Bar | 1 | 3/4″ × 1″ × 91/2″ | oak |
| D | Dowels | 2 | 3/8″ × 2″ | dowel |

the end pieces. Then drill a 3/16-inch hole in the center of each larger hole, completely through the wood. The smaller hole is for the screw, and the larger hole holds the wood plug that conceals the screw head.

Put the ends in position aligned with the bottom edge and outside corner of the base (A). Hold it in place while one partner marks the pilot-hole location on the end of the base by making pencil marks through the holes in the ends (B).

To ensure accuracy, make small starting holes for your drill by putting the point of a nail set over your pencil marks and giving it a blow with a hammer. Then drill 1/8-inch-deep pilot holes through these points.

Spread glue on the ends that will be attached to the base, and put a small amount of soap on the screws to help ease

them into the hard oak. Place the ends in position; insert and tighten the number 6, 1-inch flat-headed wood screws. When the ends are in place, put a small amount of glue on the 3/8-inch oak plugs, and insert them in all the screw holes. After the glue has dried, cut the plugs off close to the surface.

Drill a 3/8-inch hole 3/4 inch from each end of the napkin bar (C) in the 3/4-inch side. Insert a 2-inch section of doweling into each hole.

Give your napkin holder a thorough sanding with 120-grit sandpaper. Use sandpaper wrapped around a block of wood to sand plug stubs flush with the end.

We gave our napkin holder a coat of golden oak stain to highlight the grain. After the stain dried, we applied several coats of paste wax to protect the finish.

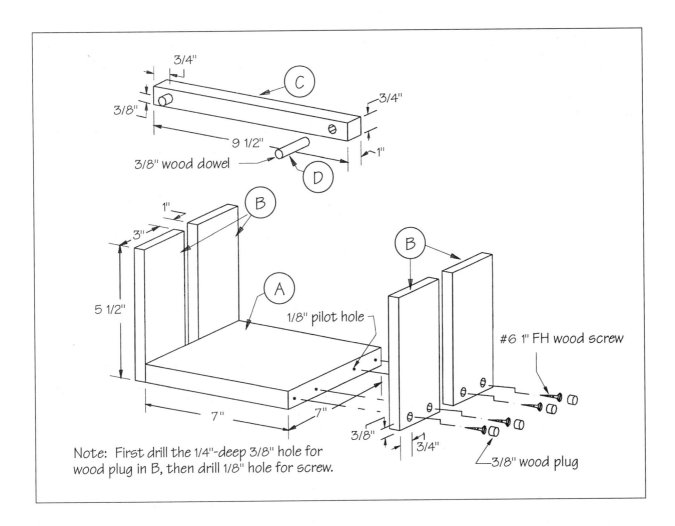

3/4"

C

3/4"

3/8"

9 1/2"

3/8" wood dowel

D

1"

1"

3"

B

A

1/8" pilot hole

B

5 1/2"

#6 1" FH wood screw

7"    7"

3/8"

3/4"

3/8" wood plug

Note:  First drill the 1/4"-deep 3/8" hole for
wood plug in B, then drill 1/8" hole for screw.

# GIFT BOXES

The early pioneers made these simple basket boxes of pine with grapevine handles. We designed ours so that you too can put them together easily and effortlessly. These boxes make ideal gifts, filled with candy or cookies, or you can use them on a dresser or dining room table. They're popular home accessories that anyone would like.

We made the boxes in two sizes. Construction is identical; both use lattice for the sides and bottom. The larger box uses grapevine for a handle; the smaller has braid handles made from heavy twine. Lattice is readily available at lumberyards, but you'll have to take a walk in the woods or go to a florist for the grapevine. We soaked our grapevine in warm water for several hours to make it soft and pliable to work with. Both the boxes have a natural finish.

Begin construction by cutting the lattice to size. The sides (B1, B2) and ends (C1, C2) of both boxes are cut from 3 1/2-inch-wide lattice. The bottom of the small box is formed by a single piece of 5 1/2-inch-wide lattice and the bottom of the large box is made from two sections of 3 1/2-inch-wide lattice. For all measurements, see the Cutting List.

For the large box, lay out the location of the handle holes on the sides (B2), measuring 7 3/4 inches from either end. Make a pencil mark, then measure 1 inch down from the top edge. Drill a 1/16-inch hole in each corner of the two ends for the handles to slip through.

For the small box, drill 3/16-inch holes in the top corners of the two end pieces, 1 inch

TIME REQUIRED

Four hours for cutting, building, and assembling both boxes, plus drying time for glue and finish.

### SHOPPING LIST: BOTH BOXES

| Item | Quantity |
| --- | --- |
| $3^1/2''$ lattice | 12' |
| $5^1/2''$ lattice | 1' |
| $7/8''$ wire brads | small box |
| carpenter's wood glue | small bottle |
| 120-grit sandpaper | 2 sheets |
| thin wire | small spool |
| heavy twine | small spool |
| grapevine | 2' |
| paint, stain, or other finish | 1/2 pint |

### CUTTING LIST: SMALL BOX

| Part | Name | Quantity | Size | Material |
| --- | --- | --- | --- | --- |
| A1 | Bottom | 1 | $1/4'' \times 5^1/2'' \times 11''$ | pine lattice |
| B1 | Sides | 2 | $1/4'' \times 3^1/2'' \times 11''$ | pine lattice |
| C1 | Ends | 2 | $1/4'' \times 3^1/2'' \times 5''$ | pine lattice |

### CUTTING LIST: LARGE BOX

| A2 | Bottom | 2 | $1/4'' \times 3^1/2'' \times 17''$ | pine lattice |
| --- | --- | --- | --- | --- |
| B2 | Sides | 2 | $1/4'' \times 3^1/2'' \times 17''$ | pine lattice |
| C2 | Ends | 2 | $1/4'' \times 3^1/2'' \times 6^1/2''$ | pine lattice |

from the side and 1 inch from the top, for the handles to slip through.

The boxes are assembled by driving two $7/8$-inch by 18 wire brads along each of the short ends of the side pieces (B), $1/8$ inch from the edge. Be careful not to split the wood. When all the nails are in place, apply glue to the shorter edges of each end piece (C), then attach the sides to the end pieces, squaring them up and nailing them together.

Drive evenly spaced wire brads every 2 inches around the edges of the bottom (A1, A2). Keep them $1/8$ inch from the edge and pound them into the wood just deep enough so their points emerge from the other side. Then turn the boxes over and apply glue to

the bottom edges of the side and end pieces (B and C). Put the bottom in place. Have one member of the team hold it square while the other drives the brads.

When the glue is dry, sand the boxes smooth. If the ends or sides overlap slightly, place a piece of sandpaper on a flat surface, and rub the end of the box over it; this will grind down high spots and leave the ends square.

If your grapevine is dry and stiff, soak it in water until it becomes pliable. Then make a loop by passing thin wire through the handle holes. Place the end of the grapevine in this loop, and pull the loop tight. Then form another loop and pull it

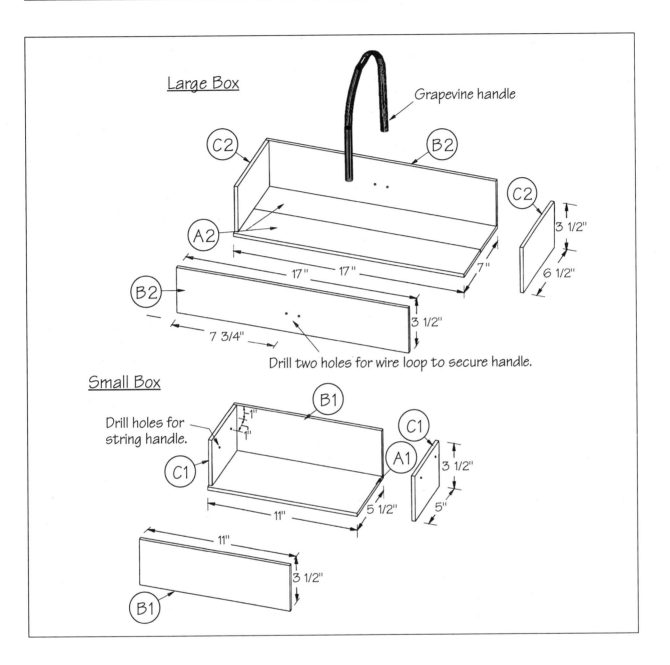

Large Box

Grapevine handle

C2
B2
C2
A2
3 1/2"
6 1/2"
17"
17"
7"
B2
7 3/4"
3 1/2"

Drill two holes for wire loop to secure handle.

Small Box

B1
Drill holes for string handle.
C1
A1
C1
3 1/2"
11"
5 1/2"
5"
11"
3 1/2"
B1

tight. Finally, wrap the wire around the loop between the grapevine and the outside of the box, and tie off and cut the wire.

Heavy packing twine was used as handles for the smaller box. For each handle, take three 12-inch-long strands, push them through one handle hole, and tie a knot inside the box. Braid the twine, pass the other end through the other hole on that end piece, and tie it off. Cut the strands neatly at the knots.

We gave the boxes a natural tung oil finish, and when it dried, we applied a coat of paste wax for protection.

# BIRD FEEDER

ere's a bird feeder sure to become a popular stopover for your feathered friends. We designed our feeder, made of redwood and acrylic window pane, to protect the feed from rain and snow and from other critters that like to ravage a stash of food.

The feeder is filled with seed from the top, which is raised and slides up the suspension ropes. A controlled amount of seed spills out through the space below the clear pane onto the deck where the birds come to feed. Because of the feeder's clear sides, you can always see the seed level and refill it when needed.

Our feeder is made from redwood available at lumberyards. Since only small pieces are required, purchase scrap pieces if possible. Pine may be substituted, but it should be stained to protect it from the weather.

Transfer the end (B) dimensions from the End Detail on the diagram to the wood. Cut two pieces to these dimensions. You could also make a full-size pattern on a piece of cardboard and then use it to mark the shape of the end on the wood. Cut the remaining pieces to length, as specified in the Cutting List.

Since redwood splits easily, use a 1/16-inch drill bit to make pilot holes for the nails. Drill two evenly spaced holes 3/8 inch from the bottom of the end pieces (B). Drill five holes spaced about 2 inches apart and 3/8 inch from the edge of one top part (C).

TIME REQUIRED

Four hours for cutting, building, and assembling, plus drying time for glue and finish.

### SHOPPING LIST

| Item | Quantity |
|---|---|
| 1×8 redwood | 1' |
| 1×6 redwood | 4' |
| acrylic window pane | 8" × 12" (minimum) |
| number 4 finishing nails (galvanized or aluminum) | small box |
| 7/8" by 18 wire brads (galvanized or aluminum) | small box |
| carpenter's wood glue | small bottle |
| 3/8" manila rope | 8' |

### CUTTING LIST

| Part | Name | Quantity | Size | Material |
|---|---|---|---|---|
| A | Base | 1 | 3/4" × 71/4" × 12" | redwood |
| B | Ends | 2 | 3/4" × 51/2" × 61/4" | redwood |
| C | Roof pieces | 2 | 3/4" × 51/2" × 12" | redwood |
| D | Sides | 2 | 1/8" × 33/8" × 9" | acrylic window pane |
| E | Bottom | 1 | 3/4" × 2" × 71/2" | redwood |

Apply glue to one end of the bottom (E), and nail on one end piece (B) with number 4 finishing nails. Turn the unit over, and glue and nail on the other end. Have one team member hold the end in position while the other does the nailing. Sink all nail heads with a nail set.

Cut sides (D) out of a piece of acrylic window pane. Acrylic can be cut with a saw or scored with a sharp knife and then broken over a table edge. Drill three evenly spaced 1/16-inch holes on each end, 3/8 inch from the edge.

The side panels (D) are then nailed flush with the top edge of the ends (B) with 7/8-inch by 18 aluminum or brass brads. This leaves a slot at the bottom for the food to pour through.

Now run a bead of glue down the top edge of one roof piece (C). Nail both roof parts together with number 4 aluminum nails. Since the edge of one top is nailed to the side of the other, the roof is 3/4 inch wider on one side. This will not bother the birds, but if you want a balanced roof either trim 3/4 inch from the long side or join the top part with a miter joint. Turn your top over, and have one team member hold it square while the other drills a 3/8-inch hole in the V 11/4 inches from each end of the roof.

Next, drill two 3/8-inch holes in the base (A) 11/4 inches from each end and centered. Mark the location of the feeder house on the base by measuring 11/2 inches from each end of the base. Put glue on the bottom edges of the feeder house, and drive nails through the center of the house to secure it to the base. You will not need pilot holes.

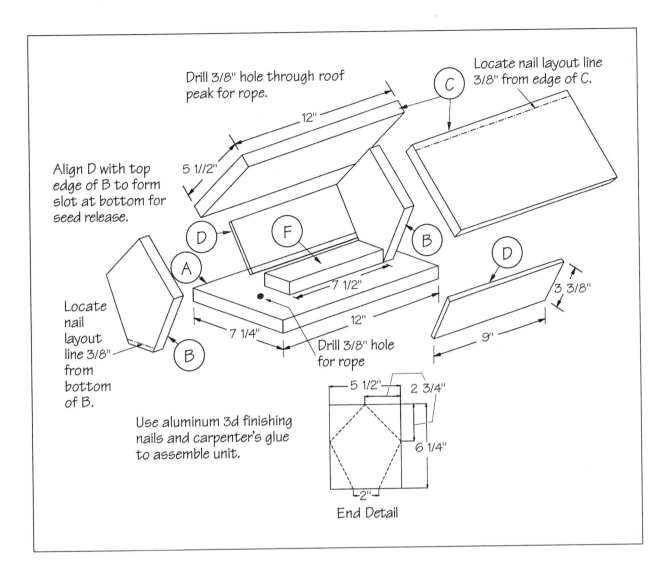

Drill 3/8" hole through roof peak for rope.

Locate nail layout line 3/8" from edge of C.

12"

5 1/2"

Align D with top edge of B to form slot at bottom for seed release.

Locate nail layout line 3/8" from bottom of B.

Use aluminum 3d finishing nails and carpenter's glue to assemble unit.

7 1/2"

7 1/4"

12"

Drill 3/8" hole for rope

3 3/8"

9"

5 1/2"    2 3/4"

6 1/4"

2"

End Detail

Measure out about 3½ feet of the rope and tie a loop in its center. Feed the ends of the rope through the holes in the roof and the base of the feeder. Tie knots in the rope under the base to hold it in place, and your feeder is ready to be filled with seed. Just lift the roof, and pour in the first serving.

# PLANT CENTER

The "green thumb" member of the family will proudly display his or her plants in this easy-to-build three-pot plant holder. We designed it around an 18-inch plastic window box liner to hold three 3-inch-diameter clay pots.

The planter is made of only four pieces of 1×6 wood. We chose redwood, but you could also use pine. Since water spills are likely, we treated our holder with a water sealer.

Redwood is soft and easy to cut. Lay out the dimensions of the sides (A) and the top and bottom (B) on the 1×6 board, following the Cutting List, and cut out the pieces.

Choose one of your B parts for the top, and lay out the location of the three pot holes. The hole centers are located 3 1/2 inches from each end (side holes) and 9 inches from either end (middle hole), centered 2 3/4 inches from either edge. Use a compass to draw a 1 1/2-inch-radius circle around each of these points. Then drill a 3/8-inch hole at a point inside each circle touching the circumference. Clamp the top to the table, and using these holes to insert

Two to three hours for cutting, building, and assembling, plus drying time for glue and finish.

## SHOPPING LIST

| Item | Quantity |
|------|----------|
| 1×6 redwood | 5″ |
| number 4 finishing nails | small box |
| carpenter's wood glue | small bottle |
| 3″ clay pots with plants | 3 |
| 120-grit sandpaper | 2 sheets |
| 4″ × 17³/4″ plastic tray | 1 |
| water sealer finish | 1 pint |

## CUTTING LIST

| Part | Name | Quantity | Size | Material |
|------|------|----------|------|----------|
| A | Sides | 2 | ³/4″ × 5¹/2″ × 5″ | redwood |
| B | Top and bottom | 2 | ³/4″ × 5¹/2″ × 18″ | redwood |

the blade of a coping saw, cut out the pot holes.

Redwood splits easily, so you'll need to use a ¹/16-inch drill to make pilot holes for the nails. Lay out the location of the pilot nail holes on the two sides (A). Use a combination square to draw two lines across the face of each side piece, one ³/8 inch and the other 3⁵/8 inches from the bottom edge. Drill three evenly spaced ¹/16-inch holes along each of these lines.

Apply glue to the end of the bottom (B), and have one team member hold it upright while the other nails on the sides (A). Drive number 4 finishing nails through the pilot holes along the bottom edge of the side into the edge of the bottom. Check that the lower edge of the side is flush with the bottom.

Put glue on the end of the top (B), and nail it in place 3¹/4 inches above the bottom. Then turn your holder over, and glue and nail on the other side. Set all nail heads below the surface of the wood with a nail set, and your plant holder is ready for service. Place the plastic liner on the base to catch any overflow.

We applied a coat of water sealer with a rag to prevent water stains. This is only for appearance, since redwood is not harmed by water and is naturally rot resistant.

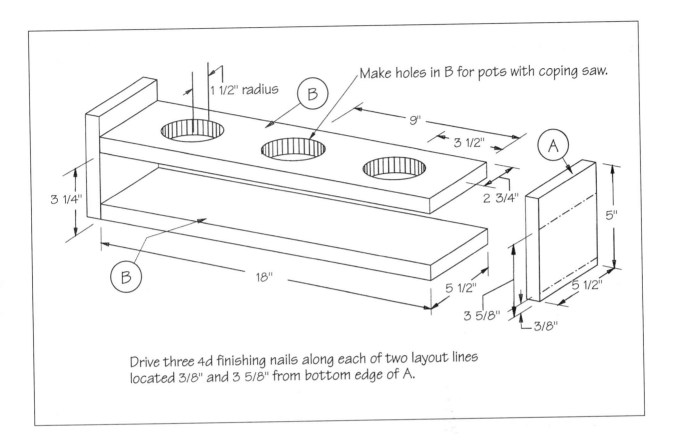

1 1/2" radius

Make holes in B for pots with coping saw.

B

9"

3 1/2"

A

2 3/4"

3 1/4"

5"

B

18"

5 1/2"

5 1/2"

5 1/2"

3 5/8"

3/8"

Drive three 4d finishing nails along each of two layout lines
located 3/8" and 3 5/8" from bottom edge of A.

# DOLL SLIDE

There is nothing more adorable than a cuddly doll, but we noticed that there's not much furniture built for them. Here's an easy-to-make slide just right for a doll 12 to 20 inches tall. A dowel hinge makes the slide collapsible for easy storage when not in use.

All materials are readily available and inexpensive. Our slide has a natural finish, but you can also spray paint it a cheery color.

Begin construction by cutting the 1-inch-wide lattice to length, following the Cutting List, to make the slide parts. Use an inexpensive wood miter box to make square cuts.

Drill a 3/16-inch hole through the center of each slide side (A). Glue then nail three of the four braces to the underside of the sides at the top, bottom, and center with 5/8-inch wire brads.

Decide which end of the slide you want to be the top. Cut the hinge dowel (F) to length, and place it across the underside of the slide frame next to the top brace. Then place the remaining brace in position next to the dowel, adjust it so that the dowel has room to move, and glue and nail the brace into place.

TIME REQUIRED

Two to three hours for cutting, building, and assembling, plus drying time for glue and finish.

### SHOPPING LIST

| Item | Quantity |
|------|----------|
| 1″ pine lattice | 15′ |
| 1/4″ dowel | 1′ |
| 120-grit sandpaper | 2 sheets |
| carpenter's wood glue | small bottle |
| 5/8″ wire brads | small box |
| posterboard or cardboard | 5″ × 24″ |
| lightweight string | 2′ |
| paint, stain, or other finish | 1 pint |

### CUTTING LIST

| Part | Name | Quantity | Size | Material |
|------|------|----------|------|----------|
| A | Slide sides | 2 | 1/4″ × 1″ × 24″ | pine lattice |
| B | Braces | 4 | 1/4″ × 1″ × 5 1/2″ | pine lattice |
| C | Ladder sides | 2 | 1/4″ × 1″ × 18″ | pine lattice |
| D | Rungs | 5 | 1/4″ × 1″ × 6″ | pine lattice |
| E | Joint braces | 2 | 1/4″ × 1″ × 2 1/4″ | pine lattice |
| F | Hinge dowels | 2 | 1/4″ × 2″ | dowel |
| G | Slide bottom | 1 | 5″ × 24″ | posterboard |

While the slide frame glue is drying, drill a 1/4-inch hole in each ladder side (C), 1 inch from one end and centered. Then drill a 3/16-inch hole in each C piece, 6 inches from the same end and centered. Next, glue and nail on the rungs (D), placing the first rung 2 inches from the bottom (the end without the holes) and spacing them 2 inches apart.

Glue and nail the joint brace (E) across the top braces of the slide frame. These pieces keep the dowel hinge in place.

Turn the slide frame over and apply glue to the face of the braces and along the sides. From the light cardboard or posterboard, cut the slide bottom (G) to size, following the Cutting List.

Your slide is easy to finish or paint while it is in two pieces. We gave ours one coat of a natural oil wipe-on finish and used a black posterboard for the slide to create a nice contrast.

When your finish is dry, assemble the slide. Place the 1/4-inch dowel in the hole in the top of your ladder, and align it with the dowel slot on the underside of the slide frame. Then push the dowel into the hole. You might have to work the dowel a little, because paint may have dripped into these holes. Flip the slide over and insert the other hinge dowel into its hole. Then fit the posterboard in place, and the slide is completely assembled.

Thread string through the holes in the center of the ladder and slide sides, and tie knots in its ends to keep it in place. Your slide will stand or can be folded flat for storage.

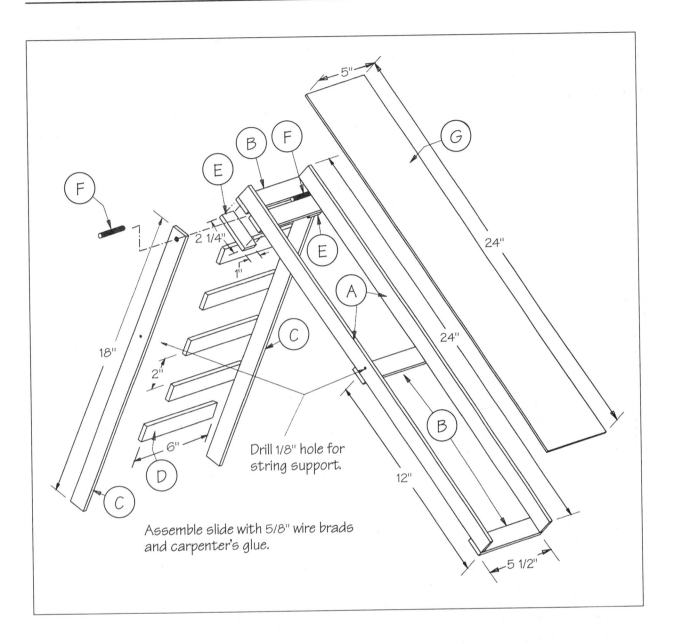

5"

F

B   F

E

G

F

2 1/4"

1"

24"

18"

A

C

24"

2"

E

6"

B

D

Drill 1/8" hole for
string support.

12"

C

Assemble slide with 5/8" wire brads
and carpenter's glue.

5 1/2"

# MAGAZINE OR RECORD RACK

This contemporary-looking rack will enhance a den or bedroom and solve the problem of storing record albums or piles of magazines. It is simple to build using dimensional lumber from a home center or lumberyard. One 3-foot piece of 1×12 lumber and some 1-inch lattice strips are all you need to construct the rack. We made ours easy to move by adding furniture casters.

Construction is fast. Cut the 1×12 into three parts for the two side pieces (A) and the bottom (B), following the dimensions on the Cutting List. Then cut the 1-inch lattice into the lengths required. Use an inexpensive miter box, and clamp a piece of scrap 14 1/4 inches from the cutting slot to act as a stop when cutting the slats. Slide the lattice through the miter box until it hits the stop, then cut it to length. This saves time, since you will not have to measure each piece.

Lay out the location of the nails with a combination square. Draw a line 3/8 inch

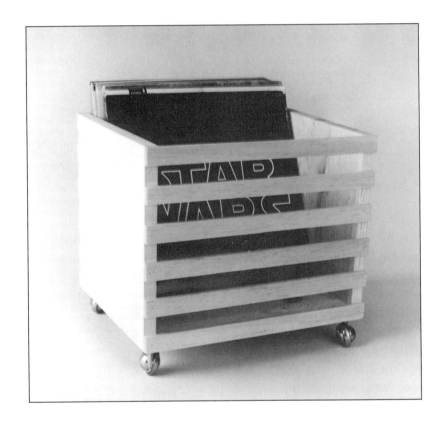

from the bottom of each side piece. Then drive four evenly spaced number 4 finishing nails along each line. Drive a 7/8-inch wire brad into both ends of each slat (C) about 3/8 inch from the end and centered. Now you are ready to assemble your rack.

Run a bead of glue down one 11 1/4-inch edge of the bottom (B). Then, have one

TIME REQUIRED

Four hours for cutting,
building, and assembling,
plus drying time for glue
and finish.

## SHOPPING LIST

| Item | Quantity |
|---|---|
| 1×12 pine | 4' |
| 1" pine lattice | 20' |
| number 4 finishing nails | small box |
| 7/8" × 18 wire brads | small box |
| carpenter's wood glue | small bottle |
| 2" casters | 4 |
| 120-grit sandpaper | 2 sheets |
| paint, stain, or other finish | 1 pint |

## CUTTING LIST

| Part | Name | Quantity | Size | Material |
|---|---|---|---|---|
| A | Sides | 2 | 3/4" × 11 1/4" × 11 | pine |
| B | Bottom | 1 | 3/4" × 11 1/4" × 13" | pine |
| C | Slats | 12 | 1/4" × 1" × 14 1/4" | pine lattice |

member of the team hold the bottom upright while the other nails one of the side pieces (A) into place. Repeat for the opposite side.

Turn your rack on its side so that the edges of the ends and bottom are in contact with the workbench or table. Put a little glue on the end of a slat, and nail it into place flush with the top edge of the sides. Do the same on the opposite side, then check that the rack sides are square.

Use a piece of scrap lattice as a spacer and glue and nail the other slats to the edges of the sides. Adjust the position of the bottom slat visually; it should be close or

flush with the lower edge of the bottom.

To add casters to your rack, turn it over, and follow the manufacturer's directions for installation. Locate the casters at the corners about 3/4 inch in from all sides. The type we purchased requires four screws. To install, put the caster in place, and mark the location of the screws. Remove the caster, and drill a 1/16-inch pilot hole for each screw. Replace the caster, and screw it in place.

We finished our rack naturally by giving it a coat of wipe-on finish. If you want a more colorful rack, paint it with two coats of high-gloss spray enamel.

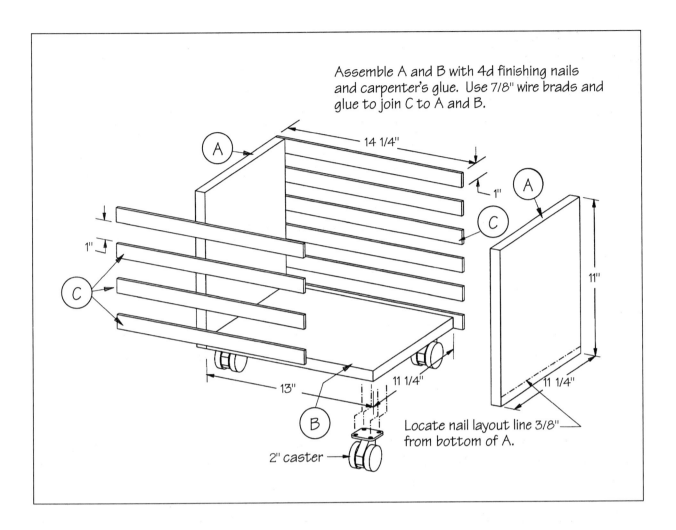

Assemble A and B with 4d finishing nails and carpenter's glue. Use 7/8" wire brads and glue to join C to A and B.

14 1/4"

1"

1"

11"

13"

11 1/4"

11 1/4"

Locate nail layout line 3/8" from bottom of A.

2" caster

# COAT TREE

Hang up your clothes! That command won't be heard as often in your house once you have one of these dandy coat trees. In a kid's room, a clothes rack like this is a colorful addition that's a lot more likely to be put to use than a hanger in the closet.

We made one and painted it with a bright, high-gloss enamel spray paint. The pole is made of 2×2 lumber and has four feet made of 1×4 stock. The hooks are 1/2-inch-diameter dowels set in holes drilled into the pole at a slight angle. Inexpensive and easy to make, the coat tree makes a handsome and useful gift.

The 2×2 lumber may be found at all home centers and lumberyards. Pick carefully through the stack, and choose a good, straight piece. You might have to purchase an extra-long 2×2 and have the yardman cut off the warped ends.

You can cut your pole to any length you want. If you are making this clothes rack for one of your apprentices, cut it for a stretching reach, since apprentices grow fast but this tree doesn't.

Cut the 1/2-inch dowel pegs (C) to 5-inch lengths. Next, lay out their location on the pole. Measure down 3 inches from the top of the pole, and make a straight line across the pole. Then mark the middle of this line

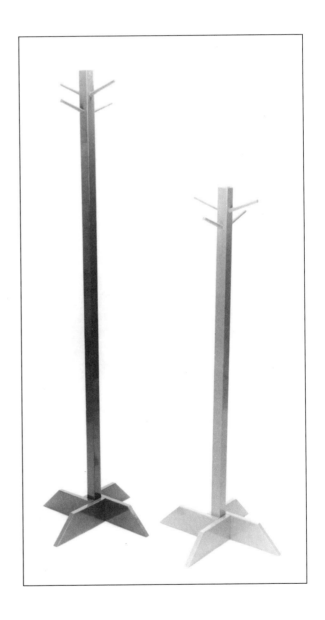

Two to three hours for cutting, building, and assembling, plus drying time for glue and finish.

| Item | Quantity |
|---|---|
| 2×2 pine | 4′ or 5′ |
| 1×4 pine | 4′ |
| 1/2″ hardwood dowel | 2′ |
| carpenter's wood glue | small bottle |
| number 4 finishing nails | small box |
| 120-grit sandpaper | 2 sheets |
| paint, stain, or other finish | 1 pint |
| cardboard (angle gauge) | cut to fit |

| Part | Name | Quantity | Size | Material |
|---|---|---|---|---|
| A | Base pieces | 4 | 3/4″ × 31/2″ × 10″ | pine |
| B | Pole | 1 | 11/2″ × 11/2″ × 4′ or 5′ | pine |
| C | Pegs | 4 | 1/2″ × 5″ | dowel |

(3/4 inch from edges). This spot is the location of your dowel hole. Use a combination square to lay out positions. Duplicate this on the opposite side of the pole. The lower peg holes are located on the other two faces of the pole, 5 inches from the top and centered. Lay these out in the same way as the upper holes.

We put our pegs in at 20-degree angles, but you can angle them as you wish. Mark your angle on a piece of cardboard, and cut it out to use for a guide when you drill.

Clamp the pole to a table, and have one member of the team hold the cardboard guide firmly along the center of the pole. Keep your 1/2-inch drill lined up with the cardboard guide, and all your holes will be drilled at the same angle. Drill the holes 3/4 inch deep.

The base pieces (A) for your coat tree are cut next. Measure down the 1×4 stock 10 inches. Then mark off a 45-degree angle back toward the end you measured from.

Cut along this line to form an angled foot. The angled piece remaining will form the next foot. Measure 10 inches from the point, and make a square cut. Repeat this process to cut the other two base pieces.

Drive three number 4 finishing nails into each base piece about 1 inch from the square end just deep enough so their points begin to come out the other side. Then put glue on the bottom 31/2 inches of one side of the pole, put the foot in place flush with the bottom and the edge of the side of the pole, and nail into place. Turn the pole, and follow the same procedure for the other three base pieces. For the last piece, extend the bottom of the pole over the end of the table.

Your dowel pegs (C) are quick and easy to install. For each dowel, place glue on one end, extending 3/4 inch up the sides, and push into a hole. After the glue has dried, sand the pole and base smooth and give your tree several coats of paint, sanding lightly between applications.

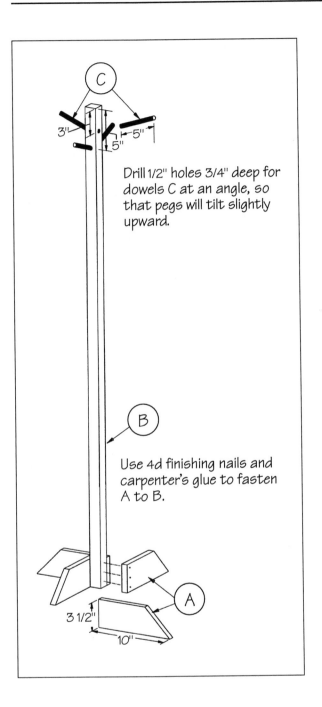

3"

5" — 5"

5"

Drill 1/2" holes 3/4" deep for dowels C at an angle, so that pegs will tilt slightly upward.

Use 4d finishing nails and carpenter's glue to fasten A to B.

3 1/2"

10"

# NAME SIGNS

Just for you or your apprentice—a personalized name board that can be hung on a bedroom door or wall. These boards can be made in a variety of ways. Here are two different versions that are easy to make.

The first design reads horizontally. It is cut from an inexpensive piece of 1×8 pine and framed with trim molding glued to its face. The 4-inch-high wooden letters are available in home centers and lumberyards. Several coats of spray paint decorate the sign board.

The second design reads vertically. It is cut from a 1×6 pine board, with angled top and bottom corners. The wood is finished naturally, and the sign is trimmed with a brightly colored ribbon glued around the outside edge. The sign hangs from a decorative hook on the top.

Basic construction is the same for both signs. Measure out the sign board (A), following dimensions on the Cutting List for the design you have chosen. Sign One has square corners, but Sign Two has corners cut at a 45-degree angle. To lay out the

angled cuts for Sign Two, measure 1¼ inches from the end and side of each corner, and mark along the edge. At each corner, draw a diagonal line connecting the two points, then cut along these lines.

Sign One is trimmed with decorative molding. Cut the top, bottom, and side trim (B and C) to length using a miter box for accuracy. If the pieces come out a little

Two to three hours for cutting, building, and assembling each sign, plus drying time for glue and finish.

### SHOPPING LIST: NAME SIGN ONE

| Item | Quantity |
|------|----------|
| 1×8 pine | 2′ |
| 1/4″ decorative hardwood molding | 7′ |
| 4″ precut letters | as needed |
| medium-size picture hangers | 2 |
| 1″ wire brads | small box |
| carpenter's wood glue | small bottle |
| 120-grit sandpaper | 2 sheets |
| spray paint | 1 can |

### CUTTING LIST: NAME SIGN ONE

| Part | Name | Quantity | Size | Material |
|------|------|----------|------|----------|
| A | Sign board | 1 | $3/4″ \times 7 1/4″ \times 24″$ | pine |
| B | Top and bottom trim pieces | 2 | $1/4″ \times 1/2″ \times 23 1/4″$ | hardwood molding |
| C | Side trim pieces | 2 | $1/4″ \times 1/2″ \times 6 3/4″$ | hardwood molding |

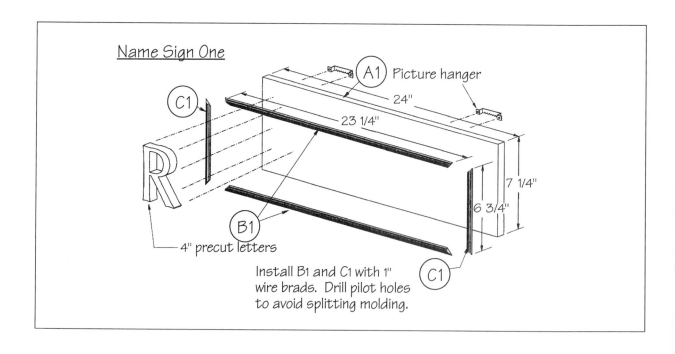

Name Sign One

Picture hanger
24"
23 1/4"
7 1/4"
6 3/4"
4" precut letters
Install B1 and C1 with 1" wire brads. Drill pilot holes to avoid splitting molding.

short, don't worry. It is important, however, that the top and bottom be the same length, and that the sides both be the same. Because the trim is hardwood, pilot holes must be drilled for the nails so that the wood won't split. The older carpenter should drill the holes, because the 1/16-inch bit needed for this breaks easily. Drill a hole

## TIME REQUIRED

Two to three hours for cutting, building, and assembling each sign, plus drying time for glue and finish.

## SHOPPING LIST: NAME SIGN TWO

| Item | Quantity |
|---|---|
| 1×6 pine | 3′ |
| 3/4″ ribbon | 6′ |
| 4″ precut letters | as needed |
| decorative hook | 1 |
| 1″ wire brads | small box |
| carpenter's wood glue | small bottle |
| 120-grit sandpaper | 2 sheets |
| spray paint | 1 can |

## CUTTING LIST: NAME SIGN TWO

| Part | Name | Quantity | Size | Material |
|---|---|---|---|---|
| A | Sign board | 1 | $3/4″ \times 51/2″ \times 291/2″$ | pine |
| B | Ribbon trim | 1 | $3/4″ \times 6′$ | ribbon |

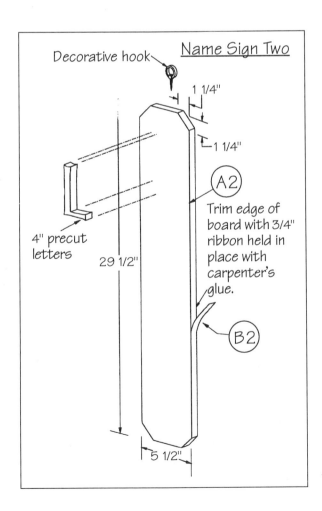

Name Sign Two

Decorative hook

1 1/4″

1 1/4″

A2

Trim edge of board with 3/4″ ribbon held in place with carpenter's glue.

4″ precut letters

29 1/2″

B2

5 1/2″

about $11/2$ inches from each end of the C pieces. Then drill a hole $11/2$ inches from each end of the B pieces and another at the center. Attach the molding to Sign One with wood glue and small finishing nails. These nails will hold the molding in place while the glue dries. Wipe off any excess glue with a rag while it is wet.

Sign Two has 3/4-inch ribbon trim around its sides attached with carpenter's wood glue. We chose a red and white decorative ribbon. Apply the glue to the sides, top, and bottom of the sign; use sparingly so that it won't soak through and stain the ribbon.

Both designs use the same precut wooden letters. Use spray paint to color them before affixing to the sign board. Several coats will be necessary, so use plenty of newspaper to protect your work surface. Open a window for proper ventilation, and don't paint in the basement near a hot-water heater or open flame because mist from a spray can is highly flammable.

When the paint has dried, use 1-inch wire brads to attach the letters. Drill 1/16-

inch pilot holes through each letter to prevent the wire beads from splitting the wood. The older team member should supervise placement.

Hanging brackets go on next. Sign One uses back-mounted picture-hanging brackets. Nail them in place with the brads that come with the brackets. Hammer carefully, making sure that the nails don't go all the way through the board.

Sign Two is held up by a decorative hook that screws into the top of the sign. Make a pilot hole for the screw by gently driving a finishing nail partway into the top and then removing it. Screw the hanger into this hole.

# LOG AND STICKS REINDEER

This charming reindeer is made entirely of firewood and kindling material. It is a perfect lawn ornament for any house during the holidays. You can make one reindeer, or fashion a herd of them once you learn the easy steps to follow.

Finding the appropriate parts for the reindeer involves walking through the woods or looking over a wood pile. It's an enjoyable job for everyone. We've noted the diameter of the wood used in the Shopping and Cutting Lists to give you an idea of the sizes of wood to look for, but don't let our dimensions stifle your creativity. You might want to use larger pieces for the body and head. Or you might decide that the antlers should be longer or more stately. That's the fun of creating your reindeer: He's a one-of-a-kind individual.

You'll note from the list that you're looking for various sizes of wood and branches, the branches being the more challenging. You need to find four of them about the same diameter for the legs, and they should be as straight as possible. Exact dimensions for the head, body, legs, and antlers don't have to be strictly followed; just try to cut the leg branches the same length.

The holes drilled for the legs are angled so that the reindeer will stand upright, and

the antlers are angled outward from the face. Use our plan as a guide for where to drill holes, but use your imagination, too. It's your reindeer!

TIME REQUIRED

Two to three hours for cutting, building, and assembling, plus drying time for glue and finish.

SHOPPING LIST

| Item | Quantity |
| --- | --- |
| plastic berries or buttons | 2 |
| carpenter's wood glue | small bottle |

CUTTING LIST

| Part | Name | Quantity | Size | Material |
| --- | --- | --- | --- | --- |
| A | Body | 1 | 6" dia. × 12" | log |
| B | Head | 1 | 4" dia. × 6" | log |
| C | Legs | 4 | 1" dia. × 24" | branches |
| D | Neck | 1 | 2" dia. × 10" | branch |
| E | Antlers | 2 | 3/4" dia. × 12" | branches |
| F | Tail | 1 | 1/4" dia. × 8" | branch |

The logs that make up the body and head can be cut to length with a regular handsaw, but a bow saw or pruning saw will make this job a lot easier. The cheeks are formed by chopping away some of the bark from each side of the head log. If you don't have a hatchet, you can cut the cheeks with a saw. Start cutting at the front of the log. Cut just below the bark, and position the saw so that it cuts at an angle toward the bark to form a V as you cut into the log.

The neck and legs fit into holes drilled in the body log. Choose the best side of your log, and drill the hole for the neck first. Use a drill bit slightly smaller in diameter than the neck branch (D). We used inexpensive spade bits and a 3/8-inch electric drill to make all the holes. The drilling should be handled by the master carpenter on this project, while the apprentice supervises the operation. Be sure to wear eye protection while drilling holes.

The neck hole is drilled at a slight forward angle, about 10 degrees. Drill this hole at least 3 inches deep, then test-fit the branch. You should have to whittle away some bark and wood to get a good, snug fit.

It is better to drill a small hole and cut the branch down to fit than to drill an oversized hole in the log and have a loose-fitting neck or leg.

Next, turn the body over, making sure that the neck hole is facing straight down, and then drill the leg holes. They are located about 1 inch from each end of the log and a couple of inches to each side of the center line. Angle the holes out about 10 degrees. Drill these four holes the same depth so that all four of the reindeer's legs will touch the ground evenly.

Use a chisel to whittle the ends of the legs until they fit in the holes, and check that each leg seats properly in its hole. Turn the reindeer over and stand him up. If the legs aren't exactly the same length, rotate them slightly in their holes. Since the leg branches are not exactly straight, turning the legs slightly is usually all that is necessary to make your reindeer stand upright.

The head is installed on the neck in the same way. Drill a hole in the bottom of the head log 1 inch or so from the back. The

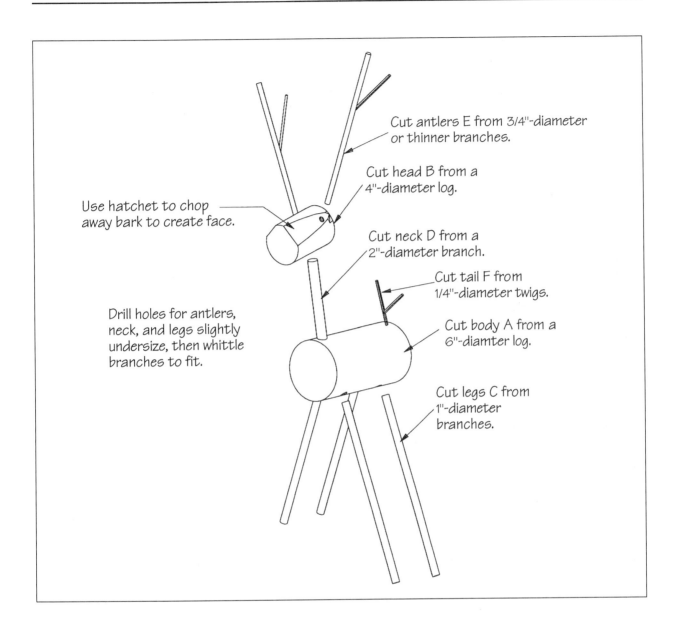

Cut antlers E from 3/4"-diameter or thinner branches.

Cut head B from a 4"-diameter log.

Use hatchet to chop away bark to create face.

Cut neck D from a 2"-diameter branch.

Cut tail F from 1/4"-diameter twigs.

Drill holes for antlers, neck, and legs slightly undersize, then whittle branches to fit.

Cut body A from a 6"-diamter log.

Cut legs C from 1"-diameter branches.

angle of the hole will determine the tilt of the head. Have one member of your team hold the head in a pleasing pose, while the other checks the angle between the head log and neck. Then turn the head log over and drill the hole. Be sure to make it undersized so that you will be assured of a tight fit after you whittle down the end of the neck.

To make the eyes, we used red plastic berries positioned in the cheek area close to the back of the head. The stems required 1/4-inch holes. Eye placement will give your reindeer its character, so move the berries around and stand back to see what the reindeer looks like with the eyes in various positions before securing them. You can also use buttons for the eyes. Buttons with shanks can be inserted in holes like the berries; for flat buttons, just glue them in place.

The antlers are made from small branches and are located above the eyes at the back of the head. Then choose a couple of branches with interesting forks to create a nice "rack" of antlers. Then drill holes slightly smaller than the diameter of the antler branches so that the branches will fit snugly. Hold them in place and drill holes at an angle to match the position wanted. The tail is made from another small branch and is installed like the other branches at the back end of the body log.

To dress your reindeer for the holidays, tie a colorful bow or bandanna around his neck.

# FILE BOX

We designed this file box for 4×6 index cards, which are a standard-size card used in offices, schools, and of course, in the kitchen for recipes.

Although the box is small in size, it is probably one of the more challenging projects. It is fun to build, however, because it uses several different materials, and the finished project is handsome and useful. The senior woodworker should not have any problems building this box, and the junior member of the team will enjoy its see-through design.

The box is made from 1/2-inch-thick oak. Many lumberyards carry this thickness, but if they don't, ask the yardman to plane down a 3/4-inch-thick 1×6 oak board; a small fee will probably be charged for the service. A dowel is used as a hinge for the acrylic top.

The sides and bottom are 51/2 inches wide, and you can cut these to length from the stock. The back is only 43/4 inches high, however, so you will have to rip (cut the length of) the board to this width and then cut it to length. When you are finished cut-

TIME REQUIRED

Eight hours for cutting, building, and assembling, plus drying time for glue and finish.

SHOPPING LIST

| Item | Quantity |
|---|---|
| $1/2'' \times 6''$ piece of oak, or oak 1×6 planed to $1/2''$ thickness | 1' |
| $3/8''$ hardwood dowel | 1' |
| $8'' \times 10''$ acrylic pane | 1 |
| number 6, 1'' wood screws (flatheaded) | 8 |
| $3/8''$ oak plugs | 8 |
| carpenter's wood glue | small bottle |
| 120-grit sandpaper | 2 sheets |
| tung oil | $1/2$ pint |

CUTTING LIST

| Part | Name | Quantity | Size | Material |
|---|---|---|---|---|
| A | Sides | 2 | $1/2'' \times 51/2'' \times 51/4''$ | oak |
| B | Bottom | 1 | $1/2'' \times 51/2'' \times 61/4''$ | oak |
| C | Back | 1 | $1/2'' \times 43/4'' \times 61/4''$ | oak |
| D | Front | 1 | $1/8'' \times 43/8'' \times 61/2''$ | acrylic |
| E | Top | 1 | $1/8'' \times 41/2'' \times 61/8''$ | acrylic |
| F | Hinge | 1 | $3/8'' \times 61/2''$ | dowel |
| G | Trim | 1 | $3/8'' \times 61/8''$ | dowel |

ting the parts to size, check that the back and bottom pieces are the same length. If they are not, the sides will not fit evenly.

The box is held together with glue and wood screws. Wood plugs are used to conceal the heads of the screws and give the box a finished appearance. You'll have to drill pilot holes for the screws to prevent them from splitting the wood. These pilot holes are located along the bottom and back edges of the side pieces (A). The centers of these holes are located $1/2$ inch in from the edges. The holes along the back edge are located $3/4$ inch down from the top and 1 inch up from the bottom, and the holes along the bottom edge are located 1 inch from the front edge and 1 inch from the back edge.

The pilot holes for the screws are $1/8$ inch in diameter and go completely through the wood. The holes for the wood plugs are $3/8$ inch in diameter and only $1/4$ inch deep. Drill the $3/8$-inch-diameter holes first, then drill the $1/8$-inch holes in the center of the larger holes.

You also have to drill pilot holes in the edges of the bottom and back pieces (B and C). Mark the location where the screw pilot holes from the sides meet the edges of the bottom and back. Then drill $1/8$-inch holes through these layout marks.

Next, make the dowel hinge hole. Turn the side parts over, and drill a $3/8$-inch-diameter hole $1/4$ inch deep in each piece, located $1/2$ inch from the top edge and $3/4$

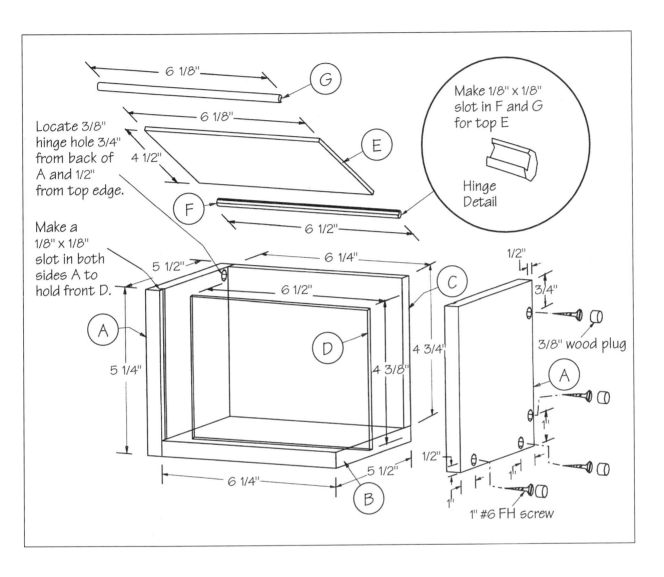

Locate 3/8" hinge hole 3/4" from back of A and 1/2" from top edge.

Make a 1/8" x 1/8" slot in both sides A to hold front D.

Make 1/8" x 1/8" slot in F and G for top E

Hinge Detail

3/8" wood plug

1" #6 FH screw

inch from the back edge. Be careful not to drill completely through the side.

The front (D) and top (E) are made from acrylic plastic that is easy to cut. Use a straight edge and a felt-tipped pen to mark the size of the front and top on the plastic sheet. The senior member of the team should use a sharp utility knife to score the plastic along the layout lines. Break the sheet along the score line by placing it over the edge of a table. Align the score line with the table edge, and then push down sharply on the sheet to snap it along the score line. When you have finished cutting these parts

to size, sand their edges to remove any sharp corners.

The dowels that form the hinge (F) and the top's front trim (G) must be slotted to fit over the edge of the top. Cut these two dowels about 7 inches long now, and after they are slotted, cut them to the exact lengths specified in the Cutting List.

The easiest way to make this slot is with a saw. Since this calls for cutting a very thin piece of wood, this job is best done by the senior woodworker. Clamp the saw in a vise with its teeth pointing up. Then hold the dowel over the saw and work it back and forth over the teeth to cut the slot. Most saws will cut a groove a bit too narrow for the acrylic; to enlarge the opening, wrap a piece of sandpaper around the edge of the acrylic top, and run it back and forth in the slot. Repeat this until the groove is large enough for the acrylic. When the top fits into the slot, trim the dowels to length. (Note that the hinge dowel is 3/8 inch longer than the trim dowel.)

Another slot must be cut along the inside of the sides, 1/4 inch back from the front edge, to hold the acrylic front. These slots are easier to cut using the saw without the vise. Clamp a side piece to your work surface, and then cut a shallow slot with the saw. Enlarge it with sandpaper wrapped over the edge of the acrylic panel.

Assembly is easy, but make sure that everything is ready, because once the sides are installed, the top cannot be removed. Glue the hinge dowel to the back edge of the top, making sure that there is an equal amount of dowel protruding from each side of the top. Then install the trim dowel on the front edge of the top, flush with the sides of the top at each end. After the glue has dried, test-fit the hinge in the hinge holes drilled in the side parts. If it is a tight fit, sand the dowel end or ends slightly as necessary.

Apply glue to one side edge of the bottom. Put the matching side in place, and check that it is flush along the bottom, front, and back; then install the number 6 screws. Apply glue on the back piece along the bottom edge and along the side edge that matches the pilot holes of the side piece just installed. Then put it in place and install the screws.

Flip the box onto the side you just installed and apply glue to the edges of the bottom and back that are facing upward. Before you install the second side piece, place the hinge dowel into the hinge hole in the first side piece. Align the dowel with the hole in the side you are installing, and push the dowel into the sides until the back, bottom, and second side piece are in full contact and flush along the edges. Then install the screws.

Occasionally move the hinged top back and forth while the glue is setting to prevent it from getting stuck in place, which can happen if any glue strayed into the hinge hole. While the glue is drying, glue the screw plugs in place. Place a couple of drops of glue in each plug hole, and tap in the plugs. Then set the box aside and allow the glue to dry.

After the glue has dried, cut off the wood plugs flush with the face of the side with a sharp chisel. Then place a sheet of sandpaper around a scrap block of wood and sand the plugs smooth. Remove any glue that may have squeezed out of the joints during assembly with your chisel. Once the box is completely sanded, it is ready to finish.

We used a wipe-on tung oil finish to show off the grain and texture of the oak. Give it three or four applications, with ample drying time in between. Put masking tape on the acrylic where it touches wood so that you will not get oil on the acrylic. Use a clean rag to spread the tung oil evenly onto all of the wood, including the interior of the file box. After the finish is dry, slide the acrylic front into the slots in the sides, and your file box is ready to use.

# TIE OR SCARF RACK

You'll have so much fun building this rack that you might just build one for everyone you know who wears a tie or scarf. It can be mounted on a closet wall or on the closet door, wherever it's most convenient.

The rack is made of maple with birch dowels and is finished in a light-colored wipe-on oil finish, which is easy to apply with a rag.

Making the sides and back is easiest if you lay them all out on a single board and bore the dowel holes before cutting out the pieces. Rip (cut lengthwise) a piece of 1/2-inch maple stock to 3 1/2 inches wide, then cut it to 24 inches long (giving you a little extra length). Photocopy the full-size pattern provided here, cut it out, and lay it on one end of the board. Draw the outline, then mark the dowel centers with a nail set through the pattern. Mark the positions for the nail pilot holes as well. Repeat for the second side by flipping the pattern upside down to produce mirror-image sides.

Bore 3/8-inch-diameter dowel holes 1/4 inch deep with a brad-point bit. To drill

these holes the same depth and avoid drilling completely through the wood, wrap a piece of tape around the drill bit 1/4 inch from its tip to act as a depth gauge. Drill until the tape touches the wood. Also bore 3/16-inch holes completely through the back for the mounting screws. Drill these holes 2

## TIME REQUIRED

Eight hours for cutting, building, and assembling, plus drying time for glue and finish.

## SHOPPING LIST

| Item | Quantity |
|---|---|
| 1/2″ × 4″ maple stock, or maple 1×4 planed to 1/2″ thickness | 2′ |
| 3/8″ dowel | 2 (3′ long) |
| number 3 finishing nails | small box |
| carpenter's wood glue | small bottle |
| 80-grit sandpaper | 1 sheet |
| 120-grit sandpaper | 1 sheet |
| paint, stain, or other finish | 1/2 pint |

## CUTTING LIST

| Part | Name | Quantity | Size | Material |
|---|---|---|---|---|
| A | Side pieces | 2 | 1/2″ × 31/2″ × 31/2″ | maple |
| B | Back | 1 | 1/2″ × 31/2″ × 14″ | maple |
| C | Dowels | 4 | 3/8″ × 141/2″ | dowel |

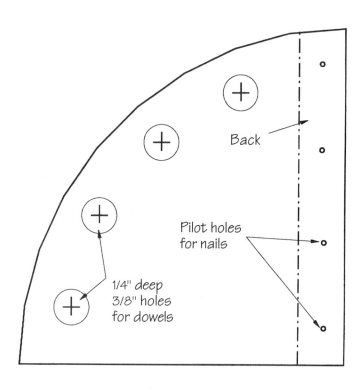

Full-Size Pattern—Tie or Scarf Rack, side B.

inches from the end of the back and 1 inch from its top edge.

Next, bore pilot holes for the brads along the back edge of the sides. If you don't have a drill bit the size of the brad, use one as a drill bit. Nip the head off a brad with a wire cutter, place it in your drill chuck, and drill the pilot holes with it.

Cut the curved parts of the sides with a coping saw, then cut the sides from the board. Clamp both pieces together, and use a sanding block or a block of wood wrapped in 80-grit sandpaper to remove the saw marks from the edges. Sand the curved sides into smooth arcs—they don't have to match the pattern exactly—then sand the surface smooth with 120-grit sandpaper. Cut the back and dowels to length, then sand all parts smooth, rounding the edges slightly.

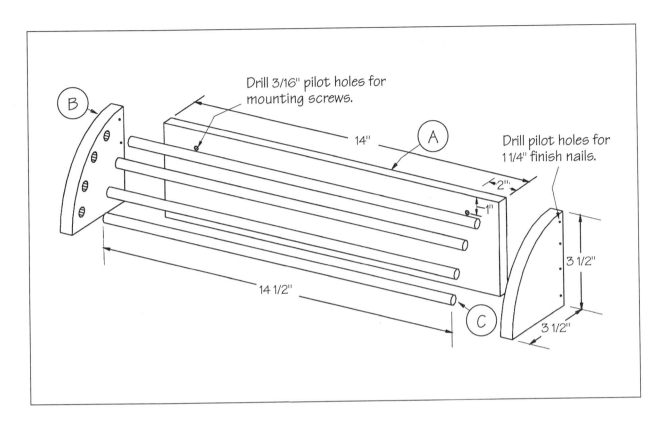

To assemble the rack, glue and nail one side to the back with 1 1/4-inch finishing nails. Apply a drop of glue to one end of each of the dowels, and insert them into the glued-up side. Put glue in the dowel holes of the second side, then glue and nail it to the back. Remove any excess glue with a damp cloth.

When the glue hardens, set the nails below the surface and fill with wood putty. When dry, sand smooth, then dust with a tack rag to remove sawdust.

To apply a wipe-on oil finish, rub it on a clean, dry cloth and spread it onto the wood. Allow the oil to penetrate the wood for five minutes or so, then wipe off the excess. Repeat the process until the maple has absorbed as much finish as possible, then buff away the excess. Allow to dry overnight, then polish with wax for more luster.

The rack should be installed with two flat-headed wood screws driven into suitable wall anchors.

# BAT ROOSTING BOX

There's a lot of misinformation about bats. Many people think they're dangerous critters, but actually, bats are one of man's best friends because they eat mosquitoes and other pesky insects. To attract bats to your backyard, make a roosting box or bat house and hang it on a tree or on your house. The box works best if it is positioned about 12 to 15 feet high. If possible, put it on the east side of the tree or house so that it will receive the morning sun but be shaded during the afternoon. Bats seem to take up residence in boxes that are protected from the wind.

The bat roosting box is easy to build using pine boards. It is designed with partitions or walls inside, which the bats attach themselves to. If the partitions are smooth, roughen them up with a chisel or saw cuts so that the bats can climb on them. Some bat experts suggest putting a band of black tape, tar paper, or paint on the front and side surfaces to attract bats to the box.

To build the bat roosting box, begin by cutting the parts to length. All the parts are

cut from 1×8 lumber. After you have cut the parts to length, trim the sides (B) so that they are 5³/4 inches wide. When you assemble the house, put the edge with the saw marks facing the back of the bat house.

Four hours for cutting, building, and assembling, plus drying time for glue and finish.

**SHOPPING LIST**

| Item | Quantity |
|---|---|
| 1×8 cedar or redwood | 8' |
| number 4 aluminum finishing nails | small box |
| large brass picture-hanging bracket | 1 |
| carpenter's wood glue | small bottle |
| 120-grit sandpaper | 1 sheet |
| black tape, tar paper, or paint | 1 pint |

**CUTTING LIST**

| Part | Name | Quantity | Size | Material |
|---|---|---|---|---|
| A | Back | 1 | $3/4'' \times 71/4'' \times 14''$ | cedar or redwood |
| B | Sides | 2 | $3/4'' \times 53/4'' \times 12''$ | cedar or redwood |
| C | Partition | 1 | $3/4'' \times 71/4'' \times 9''$ | cedar or redwood |
| D | Door | 1 | $3/4'' \times 71/4'' \times 31/2''$ | cedar or redwood |
| E | Front | 1 | $3/4'' \times 71/4'' \times 12''$ | cedar or redwood |
| F | Top | 1 | $3/4'' \times 71/4'' \times 11''$ | cedar or redwood |

Assembly is easy, but first draw layout lines on the sides to help you position your nails accurately. Make light pencil lines on the outside face of each side $3/8$ inch from the front and back edges. Then draw another line $27/8$ inches from the back edge (remember that the rough edge goes toward the back); the nails that hold the partition (C) in place go along this line. This line should extend only 9 inches down from the top edge of the side, because the partition will not run the full length of the side.

Drive five evenly spaced number 4 aluminum finishing nails along each of the longer lines and four evenly spaced nails along each of the shorter lines. Pound the nails into the wood just deep enough so their points emerge from the other side. Put some glue on the edge of the back (A), and then place a side against it. Carefully align the parts at the top, then drive the nails

through the side into the edge of the back. Next, put glue on the edge of the partition and place it in alignment with the center set of nails. Check that it is flush with the top edge of the side, and then drive the nails through the side into its edge. Install the front (E) in the same way.

Turn the unit over and apply glue to the upward-facing edges of the back, partition, and front, and nail the second side in place. Check alignment at the top and make sure that the partition is in alignment with the nails. Put the bottom (D) in place, and secure it with nails driven through the front and side into its edge.

The top (F) is glued and nailed in place with its back edge flush with the back piece (A). First, draw nail layout lines on the top piece $3/8$ inch from its back edge and $11/2$ inches from its sides. Then drive five evenly spaced nails along the back line and four nails along each side line just deep enough

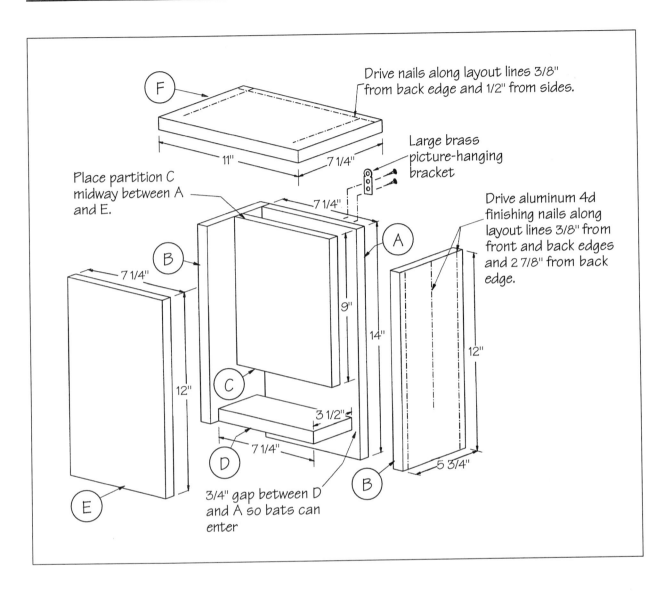

Drive nails along layout lines 3/8"
from back edge and 1/2" from sides.

Large brass
picture-hanging
bracket

Place partition C
midway between A
and E.

Drive aluminum 4d
finishing nails along
layout lines 3/8" from
front and back edges
and 2 7/8" from back
edge.

7 1/4"

7 1/4"

7 1/4"

9"

14"

12"

12"

3 1/2"

7 1/4"

5 3/4"

3/4" gap between D
and A so bats can
enter

F

B

A

C

D

B

E

so their points emerge from the other side. Apply glue to the top edges of the house assembly, and nail the roof in place.

You can stain the house with any outdoor-type stain, but we don't recommend painting it because paint will eventually peel. We gave our house a coating of water seal and left it natural. Install a large brass picture hanger on the back of the bat house, and it's ready for tenants.

# TWIG TREE

We priced these charming table decorations and found that even the smallest trees are rather expensive. To make one yourself, the cost is minimal, because the materials are provided by Mother Nature herself. The tree is a year-round decoration that can be decorated with miniature homemade paper ornaments. For Easter, make colorful paper eggs to hang from its branches; for Halloween, make tiny pumpkins and ghosts; and at Christmastime, use miniature ornaments and candy, plus miniature lights.

The tree is built using a straight tree branch as the trunk, with branches and smaller-diameter twigs nailed into the trunk to form its branches.

This is a good do-it-together project for a team, because while one person nails the branches to the tree trunk, the other can hold the trunk steady and cut twigs to size. This is also the type of project where you get to express your creativity. We encourage you to use the Cutting List only as a guide. Make your tree out of any branches that are readily available.

The base is made from pine lattice, which is available at lumberyards and home centers. Cut the base (A) to length, and apply a bit of glue to the center of one base.

TIME REQUIRED

Eight hours for cutting, building, and assembling, plus drying time for glue and finish.

SHOPPING LIST

| Item | Quantity |
|---|---|
| 1⅝″ lattice | 3′ |
| 4d box nail | 1 |
| 1/2″ wire brads | small box |
| 1″ wire brads | small box |
| carpenter's wood glue | small bottle |

CUTTING LIST

| Part | Name | Quantity | Size | Material |
|---|---|---|---|---|
| A | Base pieces | 2 | 1/4″ × 1⅝″ × 12″ | pine lattice |
| B | Feet | 2 | 1/4″ × 1⅝″ × 1⅝″ | pine lattice |
| C | Braces | 4 | 1/2″ dia. × 5″ | tree branch |
| D | Trunk | 1 | 3/4″ dia. × 10″ | tree branch |
| E | Branches | large pile | 4″ to 10″ twigs | tree branches |

Then place the other part perpendicular to the first on the glue spot. Cut the feet (B) to size, apply glue to one side, and install them under the ends of the top base leg. These feet hold the base level. Check that the base parts cross at a 90-degree angle, and place something heavy on the joint until the glue is dry.

The tree trunk (D) is made from a branch about 3/4 inch in diameter. The braces (C) are made from slightly smaller branches. For a 14-inch-tall tree, we used a trunk about 10 inches tall and braces about 5 inches long. Cut the ends of the braces to 45-degree angles so that they will fit nicely against the base and trunk. Use a miter box if possible; otherwise you can eyeball these cuts.

The trunk is held to the base with glue and a 4d box nail driven through the center of the base into the bottom of the trunk. Apply a little glue to the end of the trunk before you nail it in place.

The braces are installed with glue and 1-inch wire brads. It is easier to nail into the

trunk if you place it on a firm work surface. As you install the braces and especially the branches, do the nailing with the upper part of the trunk resting on the table and the base end supported by the helper. Nail through the braces into the trunk and into the base. If the brads come out the underside of the base, bend their points over with your hammer.

The branches are added from the base working toward the top. Start with the larger branches. Trim them to rough size, then begin gluing and nailing them to the trunk. Once you get your system going, the branches will go on quickly. To attach a branch, first drive a brad through the wood until its point just begins to come out the other side, then add a few drops of glue to the point of the nail. Place the branch on the trunk, hold it in place, and then drive the nail into the trunk. Turn the trunk a few degrees and start again. Work your way around the tree, spiraling upward toward the top.

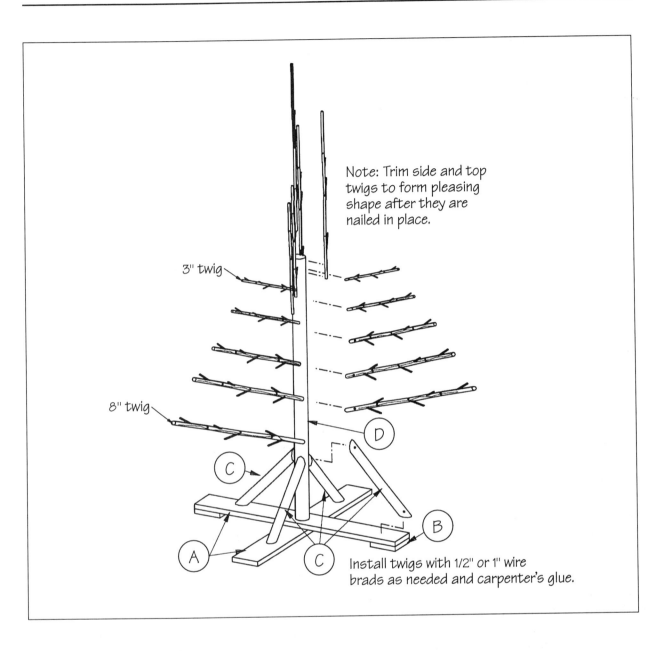

Note: Trim side and top twigs to form pleasing shape after they are nailed in place.

3" twig

8" twig

A

B

C

D

Install twigs with 1/2" or 1" wire brads as needed and carpenter's glue.

Stop occasionally and assess your work. You can trim the tree to a pleasing shape after it is all together; just check now to see that you have not left any large bare spots.

When you get within a couple of inches of the top, glue and nail the small branches vertically to the trunk. Put the taller ones on first, then work outward. You can angle some of the outer branches away from the trunk to fill in any gaps between the last row of horizontal branches and the vertical top set.

After all the branches are in place, set the tree on its base and trim it to shape with a pair of pruning shears.

# GLOSSARY

**acrylic**—a clear synthetic material that comes in sheets; used in windows instead of glass

**actual size**—the measurement of something as it exists

**align**—to bring parts of a project into a straight line

**aluminum nail**—a lightweight, stainless, and rustproof nail

**anchor**—a type of fastener used to secure something to a wall

**apprentice**—a person who works under a skilled craftsperson while learning a trade

**bar clamp**—a bar or metal rod with clamps that adjust; holds two large glued pieces of wood together

**bead**—a thin application of glue or other adhesive

**bore**—to make a hole in or through wood with a drill

**box nail**—a narrow nail with a wide head; used for nailing thin wood close to the edge

**brad**—a finishing nail less than 1 inch long

**clamp**—to hold two glued pieces of wood together while the glue dries

**countersink**—a recess below the surface of wood to receive the head of a nail, screw, or bolt

**cutout**—a design cut out of wood or to be cut out

**dimensional lumber**—standardized sizes of lumber

**dowel**—a round piece of wood that is sold in various diameters

**finishing nail**—a slender nail with a small head that does not protrude out of wood; its size is denoted by a number plus the letter *d,* e.g., 3d; the smaller the number, the shorter the nail

**flakeboard**—a composition board made of flakes and particles of wood bonded together with a synthetic resin; also called particleboard or chipboard

**flush**—the alignment of two components together so that the surfaces are even and form a continuous plane

**furring**—a thin strip of wood

**galvanized nail**—a nail that has been treated to prevent rusting

**hardwood**—wood that is dense and difficult to cut, such as oak or maple

**jig (with guide holes)**—a device used as a guide for a tool or as a template

**knot**—a variation in wood grain that is hard and often looks like a blemish

**laminate**—to build up layers of wood with glue, forming an interesting cross-section of end grain when cut

**lattice**—narrow strips of $1/4$-inch thick pine of varying widths

**layout lines or marks**—marks showing how and where pieces of a woodworking project go together

**miter cut**—a cut made at an angle so that two pieces of board can be joined to form an angle

**nominal size**—the dimension of lumber after sawing but before being planed

**parting stop**—a small wood piece used in double-hung windows

**partition**—a dividing section or segment

**peg hole**—a hole in wood the right size for a peg

**perimeter**—the combined lengths of all the sides of a piece or a project

**pilot hole**—a preliminary small guide hole to help in placement and drilling of holes in a woodworking project

**plug**—a small, pointed wooden peg pushed into a hole in wood

**radius**—the distance from the center of a circle to its circumference

**rip**—to cut a board lengthwise

**roofing nail**—a thick nail with a wide head used for attaching asphalt roofing to wood underlayment; it is often used for woodworking projects made with thick wood and that will be subjected to rugged use

**score**—to partially cut or mark with a sharp tool before cutting

**scrap**—an unneeded piece of wood that may be used as a guide, to hold pieces of a project together, or to protect wood from the blows of a tool

**softwood**—wood that is soft to the touch and easy to nail into, such as pine

**splintering**—the splitting or breaking of wood into slivers

**square cut**—a straight end cut made on a board

**stock**—commonly used and available wood pieces

**stop block**—a piece of wood used as a guide for length when sawing multiple pieces of wood to the same size

**tack**—to fasten wood pieces together loosely

**template**—a pattern to follow for a piece of a project

**waste side**—the cutoff part of a piece of wood

# ▪ Metric Conversions ▪

## INCHES TO MILLIMETRES

| IN. | MM | IN. | MM |
|---|---|---|---|
| 1 | 25.4 | 51 | 1295.4 |
| 2 | 50.8 | 52 | 1320.8 |
| 3 | 76.2 | 53 | 1346.2 |
| 4 | 101.6 | 54 | 1371.6 |
| 5 | 127.0 | 55 | 1397.0 |
| 6 | 152.4 | 56 | 1422.4 |
| 7 | 177.8 | 57 | 1447.8 |
| 8 | 203.2 | 58 | 1473.2 |
| 9 | 228.6 | 59 | 1498.6 |
| 10 | 254.0 | 60 | 1524.0 |
| 11 | 279.4 | 61 | 1549.4 |
| 12 | 304.8 | 62 | 1574.8 |
| 13 | 330.2 | 63 | 1600.2 |
| 14 | 355.6 | 64 | 1625.6 |
| 15 | 381.0 | 65 | 1651.0 |
| 16 | 406.4 | 66 | 1676.4 |
| 17 | 431.8 | 67 | 1701.8 |
| 18 | 457.2 | 68 | 1727.2 |
| 19 | 482.6 | 69 | 1752.6 |
| 20 | 508.0 | 70 | 1778.0 |
| 21 | 533.4 | 71 | 1803.4 |
| 22 | 558.8 | 72 | 1828.8 |
| 23 | 584.2 | 73 | 1854.2 |
| 24 | 609.6 | 74 | 1879.6 |
| 25 | 635.0 | 75 | 1905.0 |
| 26 | 660.4 | 76 | 1930.4 |
| 27 | 685.8 | 77 | 1955.8 |
| 28 | 711.2 | 78 | 1981.2 |
| 29 | 736.6 | 79 | 2006.6 |
| 30 | 762.0 | 80 | 2032.0 |
| 31 | 787.4 | 81 | 2057.4 |
| 32 | 812.8 | 82 | 2082.8 |
| 33 | 838.2 | 83 | 2108.2 |
| 34 | 863.6 | 84 | 2133.6 |
| 35 | 889.0 | 85 | 2159.0 |
| 36 | 914.4 | 86 | 2184.4 |
| 37 | 939.8 | 87 | 2209.8 |
| 38 | 965.2 | 88 | 2235.2 |
| 39 | 990.6 | 89 | 2260.6 |
| 40 | 1016.0 | 90 | 2286.0 |
| 41 | 1041.4 | 91 | 2311.4 |
| 42 | 1066.8 | 92 | 2336.8 |
| 43 | 1092.2 | 93 | 2362.2 |
| 44 | 1117.6 | 94 | 2387.6 |
| 45 | 1143.0 | 95 | 2413.0 |
| 46 | 1168.4 | 96 | 2438.4 |
| 47 | 1193.8 | 97 | 2463.8 |
| 48 | 1219.2 | 98 | 2489.2 |
| 49 | 1244.6 | 99 | 2514.6 |
| 50 | 1270.0 | 100 | 2540.0 |

The above table is exact on the basis: 1 in. = 25.4 mm

## U.S. TO METRIC
1 inch = 2.540 centimetres
1 foot = .305 metre
1 yard = .914 metre
1 mile = 1.609 kilometres

## METRIC TO U.S.
1 millimetre = .039 inch
1 centimetre = .394 inch
1 metre = 3.281 feet or 1.094 yards
1 kilometre = .621 mile

## INCH-METRIC EQUIVALENTS

| FRACTION | CUSTOMARY (IN.) | METRIC (MM) | FRACTION | CUSTOMARY (IN.) | METRIC (MM) |
|---|---|---|---|---|---|
| | 1/64——.015 | 0.3969 | | 33/64——.515 | 13.0969 |
| 1/32——.031 | | 0.7938 | 17/32——.531 | | 13.4938 |
| | 3/64——.046 | 1.1906 | | 35/64——.546 | 13.8906 |
| 1/16——.062 | | 1.5875 | 9/16——.562 | | 14.2875 |
| | 5/64——.078 | 1.9844 | | 37/64——.578 | 14.6844 |
| 3/32——.093 | | 2.3813 | 19/32——.593 | | 15.0813 |
| | 7/64——.109 | 2.7781 | | 39/64——.609 | 15.4781 |
| 1/8——.125 | | 3.1750 | 5/8——.625 | | 15.8750 |
| | 9/64——.140 | 3.5719 | | 41/64——.640 | 16.2719 |
| 5/32——.156 | | 3.9688 | 21/32——.656 | | 16.6688 |
| | 11/64——.171 | 4.3656 | | 43/64——.671 | 17.0656 |
| 3/16——.187 | | 4.7625 | 11/16——.687 | | 17.4625 |
| | 13/64——.203 | 5.1594 | | 45/64——.703 | 17.8594 |
| 7/32——.218 | | 5.5563 | 23/32——.718 | | 18.2563 |
| | 15/64——.234 | 5.9531 | | 47/64——.734 | 18.6531 |
| 1/4——.250 | | 6.3500 | 3/4——.750 | | 19.0500 |
| | 17/64——.265 | 6.7469 | | 49/64——.765 | 19.4469 |
| 9/32——.281 | | 7.1438 | 25/32——.781 | | 19.8438 |
| | 19/64——.296 | 7.5406 | | 51/64——.796 | 20.2406 |
| 5/16——.312 | | 7.9375 | 13/16——.812 | | 20.6375 |
| | 21/64——.328 | 8.3384 | | 53/64——.828 | 21.0344 |
| 11/32——.343 | | 8.7313 | 27/32——.843 | | 21.4313 |
| | 23/64——.359 | 9.1281 | | 55/64——.859 | 21.8281 |
| 3/8——.375 | | 9.5250 | 7/8——.875 | | 22.2250 |
| | 25/64——.390 | 9.9219 | | 57/64——.890 | 22.6219 |
| 13/32——.406 | | 10.3188 | 29/32——.906 | | 23.0188 |
| | 27/64——.421 | 10.7156 | | 59/64——.921 | 23.4156 |
| 7/16——.437 | | 11.1125 | 15/16——.937 | | 23.8125 |
| | 29/64——.453 | 11.5094 | | 61/64——.953 | 24.2094 |
| 15/32——.468 | | 11.9063 | 31/32——.968 | | 24.6063 |
| | 31/64——.484 | 12.3031 | | 63/64——.984 | 25.0031 |
| 1/2——.500 | | 12.7000 | 1——1.000 | | 25.4000 |